7 RULES TO 7 FIGURES

This book is being given to:

_____

Because I care about you and your greater success

7 RULES TO
7 FIGURES

THE ENTREPRENEUR'S PLAYBOOK TO
FREEDOM, FAMILY, AND FORTUNE

PETER VOOGD

LIONCREST
PUBLISHING

7 RULES TO 7 FIGURES
The Entrepreneur's Playbook to Freedom, Family, and Fortune

ISBN   HARDCOVER: 978-1-5445-2153-4
          PAPERBACK: 978-1-5445-2152-7
          EBOOK: 978-1-5445-2151-0

CONTENTS

INTRODUCTION

WELCOME TO THE NEW ECONOMY

WHAT DOES IT MEAN TO BE WORLD-CLASS?

To some, it might mean living a lavish lifestyle filled with vacations, unlimited income, and fame. To others, it could simply mean rising to the top in their chosen industry.

Regardless of your personal definition, being World-Class is about much more than material objects, recognition, or being the best at what you do. It's about creating an amazing lifestyle that provides all of those things but doesn't require you to sacrifice your freedom or values along the way. It's about building a thriving business that works for YOU, rather than you working for it. We've been led to believe that we can't "have our cake and eat it too," and I'm here to tell you that's wrong. In fact, I am proof of it. I've gone through fifteen years of ups and downs, spent over a quarter of a million dollars on personal growth, trained over 10,000 people, and interviewed over 300 millionaires. The biggest thing I've learned is that much of what we've been told about work-life balance is wrong. You don't have to give up everything to get what you want; you just have to know how to pursue it.

Since the release of my first book, *6 Months to 6 Figures* in 2014, my life has changed in ways I never could have imagined. I've traveled the world and shared the stage with some of the most iconic entrepreneurs, including Gary Vaynerchuk, Tim Ferriss, Les Brown, Eric Thomas, Mel

Robbins, Robert Herjavec, and more. Over 50,000 people have taken our courses, trainings, and workshops. The Game Changers Academy has exploded with new members who've collectively generated tens of millions of dollars, and they've also been featured in both *Forbes* and *Entrepreneur* magazines. We're impacting millions of people each month through our social media channels. I co-wrote a best-selling journal, *Achieving Autonomy*, grew my real estate portfolio, and most importantly, married the woman of my dreams. Since then, I've become a father, and I've been able to find the sweet spot of continuous growth and impact without losing myself along the way. I can honestly say I've never felt more at peace with my life, myself, and my business. And I can only hope that through the information provided in this book, I can help you achieve the same.

On the contrary, I would be lying if I said that this newfound success came easy. It took an unbelievable amount of dedication and focus that often resulted in bouts of anxiety, questioning myself, and the unavoidable effects of "imposter syndrome." I don't say this to discourage you, but rather to set a tone of honesty that I hope rings clear throughout the entire book. You won't find any life hacks or quick shortcuts that many of today's "gurus" claim to have. You will, however, find the roadmap I employed to achieve World-Class status, and how you choose to absorb and utilize this information is ultimately within your hands.

Running a business in today's modern world is a continuous battle, and the first step to building a life and business on your terms is learning to approach a new venture with an adaptable mindset. We're living in the age of the new economy; the way in which we conduct business, interact with others, promote our brand, and gain an audience is on an ever-changing frequency. The last two decades have arguably seen more development than any others in the history of our civilization, especially in the fields of business and technology. We've moved from the massive floppy disk to micro USBs in an extremely short amount of time. Think back to the year 2000. It doesn't seem that far off, does it? Now, imagine trying to run your business or even maintaining communication today the same way we did back then. For some of us, that would mean using a landline rather than a cell phone or relying on the postal service rather than lightning-fast email or social media platforms. Even the phrase "app" wasn't attached to a technological meaning but used to reference the snack we consumed before a meal.

Suffice it to say, technology has changed our lives in major ways. Consider these other advances:

- You can use both a landline and the internet at the same time
- You can fast-forward through commercials or pay to omit commercials all-together
- You can have dinner, groceries, and alcohol delivered to you within the hour, just by using a few apps on your phone
- You no longer have to leave your couch to watch a new movie; you can just rent it through one of many available streaming services
- You can purchase practically anything you desire and have it delivered as early as the following day
- You no longer have to memorize phone numbers
- Most communication is done via text, and it's rare to receive a voicemail
- Most of the population, including children, have smartphones, with no memory of Nokia
- We can decide whether or not to date someone simply by swiping left or right
- We no longer have to worry about physical photos being damaged because we have access to them right on our phones
- You can create your own music playlists on your phone or have an app create one for you
- Wi-Fi is readily available wherever you go

So, what do all of these changes mean for the modern-day entrepreneur? It means much of what we were previously taught no longer applies, even if it was as recent as five to ten years ago. The old economy is gone, and it's never coming back. We are living in a "now or never" society, one that requires you to immediately adapt or be left behind. Age no longer determines a person's ability to be successful, and soon, neither will your experience level. I personally know sixteen- and seventeen-year-olds who are worth millions and previously successful fifty-year-olds who are now dead broke.

HOW DOES THAT EVEN HAPPEN?

From what I've seen, failure often comes from an unwillingness to adapt and a "my way or the highway" mentality. You often hear people say things like, "I have twenty years of experience; I should be paid more," but in actuality, that person has one year of experience repeated twenty times over. If they're not sharpening their skills, learning better tools, or constantly trying to better themselves, then you could even say those twenty years are no longer relevant. That experience doesn't offer anything useful in modern-day times, so why should they expect more money or more success? Age or time doesn't guarantee a higher income. It's about providing relevant value to the marketplace and understanding supply and demand.

This is not the time to back down or be a follower. This is the time to step up and lead—to lean into the new economy and take advantage of every opportunity or resource, no matter how foreign they may seem. Now is the time to wake up and see the future right in front of you. Once you do, you'll realize this is quite possibly the greatest time in human history to be alive. We are part of the biggest culture shift that's ever existed. This shift has already begun and is speeding up with each passing day. I don't want you to miss out on the tremendous opportunities the new economy brings to those who are hungry enough to listen, learn, and most importantly, execute. My singular focus is to make sure you're a part of this HUGE wave of success. It is not too late, for now. The first adopters are perfectly positioned to succeed at a whole new level.

This book is about YOU. Your results. Your future. Your income. Your story. Your legacy. I won't take up too much time talking about myself. However, I do want you to know who I am, how I can help you, and the importance of living a life on YOUR terms. You must realize you're either building your ideal lifestyle or helping somebody else build theirs. I was fortunate enough to learn at a young age to never let someone who's given up on their dreams talk you out of yours.

I wasn't supposed to be successful. I grew up in a small town on the Oregon Coast, with a population of around 6,200 people. Nobody around me had money, and there were very few, if any, true entrepreneurs that I could talk with or look up to. If you had told me I was going to make six figures by age twenty-three and become a millionaire by twenty-eight, I would have laughed in your face. I always felt judged, which made me feel like an outcast, causing me to rebel. I was the kid that everybody else's parents told their kids not to hang out with. These experiences shaped my "against the grain" mentality.

My first taste of entrepreneurship came when I was just fifteen years old and started selling shoes on eBay. It was a way for me to differentiate from what everybody else was doing. I started by selling Air Jordans and eventually bought merchandise in bulk and sold bigger items. The fact that I could put something online and sell it to someone in a different state was mind-blowing, and it quickly became an obsession that brought me to where I am today.

In fact, I remember the specific moment in time when I realized the true economic power of the internet. A group of friends came over to do a hired labor job for my father, which consisted of hauling buckets of sand up and down a large hill. With the prospect of being paid, I was initially on board to participate, but the constant thought of how my shoes were doing on eBay kept nagging at me, impacting my motivation for the boring tasks at hand. I made up an excuse to get out of the work, ran inside to check my listing, and was baffled to see I had made $91 in just a few short hours. Then, I calculated how much each of my friends made working eight hours for my dad, and it was just $63. That's when I knew I would never work a normal job, and this newfound entrepreneurial bug had me hooked. I would spend the rest of my life exploring the endless capabilities of the internet.

I also had a stark realization years later that's of vital importance to understand as an entrepreneur: The money I made that day didn't just come from the effort of posting and selling a pair of shoes. It came from taking a risk that most were too oblivious to see or didn't want to take.

As you journey into becoming the best version of yourself, don't lose sight of who you are and where your journey began. Having an acute level of self-awareness will make those future struggles and ebbs and flows of technological shifts far easier to bear. It will also allow you to adapt to fluctuation and recognize potential faults, rather than waste time and energy searching for a solution that may or may not exist. That's ultimately where the journey of becoming a World-Class human begins, and I'm both excited and honored to help you through this phase of your pursuit.

Whether you've already made your first million, or you're looking to transition into entrepreneurship, or you've been struggling as an entrepreneur, this book will serve as a roadmap to help you become the best at what you do, both personally and financially. In turn, you'll not only reach financial freedom, but you'll do it in a way that allows you to live a World-Class life.

The process of starting a business isn't difficult; millions of new businesses are started each year. The real work comes in the process of building a business to generate sustainable, ongoing income. You must be willing to put in the time, think outside the box, and scale the cliff of uncertainty with an almost blinding level of confidence. Entrepreneurs with the ability to thrive at this highest level are not a rare breed; they just do things that most aren't willing to do. They have an uncanny ability to adapt and adjust to what's ahead. Over and over again.

Real entrepreneurship is committing yourself before you have the guarantee of success. I truly believe that time is life's most precious commodity, and I value your time at the highest level, so I've simplified this book. I've taken out anything I felt wasn't extremely valuable to you. I could have made this 300+ pages long, and I could have made myself feel smarter than I really am by adding more content, more elaborate stories, and more details, but I'm big on keeping things simple. Complexity is the enemy of execution. Many of the books I've read in the past could have gotten their point across and been just as valuable (if not more) had they cut out 60 percent of the fluff, wasted words, and BS.

If you're someone who avidly reads about entrepreneurship, you know that most business-related books have a similar focus: make money fast while doing very little. As great as that sounds, you've likely realized that it's just a little too good to be true. The insight tends to be too general, is often outdated, and filled with a lot of unusable fluff. That is unless you're currently sitting on a pile of disposable cash.

I considered those factors when writing this book and ultimately decided to take a new approach. Not only will we cover proven tactics and strategies for generating income, we'll also look inward and work to acknowledge any habits or mindsets that might be holding you back from accessing your true, inner greatness. My hope isn't to provide you with quick tips and tricks that will become irrelevant in six months. It's to teach you to approach entrepreneurship with your entire self: mind, body, and soul. It's to help you build a solid, unbreakable foundation, resulting in ongoing, sustainable wealth and freedom.

Now, don't get me wrong; this book won't be the perfect solution to all of your problems. Your success will ultimately rely on the work you're willing to put in. However, if I'm able to help you figure out your next move and ensure you put intention behind every action from here on out, then I've done my job. Life is about adapting and adjusting consistently, and once you learn that chaos is almost guaranteed, you'll learn to accept it and maneuver through it efficiently. Once you learn to approach uncertainty as an opportunity to sharpen your perspective rather than an unmanageable setback, that's when you'll be within arm's reach of living life on your terms.

BUT FIRST, A WORD OF WARNING

Building a World-Class lifestyle in today's new economy comes with challenges, and these challenges often aren't what you'd expect. They're not just the business and financial challenges every entrepreneur faces when starting or growing their business. They're the hidden challenges that sneak up on you *after* you start to experience success.

This is why we see people all too often achieve massive success in one area, only to fall massively short in another. This often leads to regret, and if you've talked to anyone who has regret, you know it stings.

So, if you've built a $100 million business but you don't have a lifestyle you're inspired by and proud of, you did it all wrong.

If you've built a fan base of millions, sold out arenas, and achieved superstardom but sold your soul in the process, you did it all wrong.

If you've become the number-one sales rep in your company but sacrificed your health, you did it all wrong.

If you've become a *NYTimes* best-selling author but cheated on your wife and slept with multiple women, you did it all wrong.

If you've built a successful startup and raised millions of dollars but left a trail of failed relationships behind you, you did it all wrong.

If you've started a business and have tons of employees, but you work eighty hours a week and miss all your kids' events because your business controls you, you did it all wrong.

If you've become an exceptional CEO but you're a horrible parent and your kids don't know who you are, you did it all wrong.

You must be aware of these situations and challenges and prepare for them. If not, you risk ruining your life in the attempt to build a better one. I know that might sound harsh, but I've seen it happen too many times to count. And in a world filled with BS, sometimes the things you don't want to hear are the things you need to hear the most. Society causes people to sell themselves short in almost every area of their lives, and most people are living incongruently. Most give up too easily, have more debt than income, complain more than they hustle, and don't live a life on their terms.

This book will teach you how to overcome those struggles, own up to your faults, and set you on the path toward building an extraordinary life. If you're hanging on to old ways and not adapting to the new, you are leaving enormous amounts of potential untapped.

A few areas we'll focus on in the book include:

- The silent killer that destroys most entrepreneurs before they even start
- The untold truths of becoming a true, new-age Game Changer
- How to master the art of self-awareness and get to know yourself at a deeper level
- How to attain healthy wealth habits and achieve financial freedom

- The hidden opportunity cost of unhealthy addictions
- The hustle and grind tactics of today's top entrepreneurs
- The three game-changing moves to network in the digital era
- The power of building a brand and positioning yourself as a leading authority
- How to create maximum profits while building sustained wealth
- Mastering World-Class health, energy, and peace of mind
- Establishing a plan for real productivity, efficiency, and longevity

My ultimate goal in writing this book is to provide you with a suite of tools and strategies you can reference throughout your entrepreneurial journey—a proven playbook that will give you a massive competitive advantage, regardless of the economy. In challenging and uncertain times, you want every advantage you can get, especially in life and business. Gaining a competitive advantage isn't easy, but the upside is that it outweighs the tough times.

There is nothing worse than living a life somebody else designed for you or letting others' expectations of you become your reality. The system is designed for the majority to fail, which is exactly what they are doing. However, if you organize your life around a strong set of standards and apply the principles outlined in this book, you'll NEVER sell yourself short again; you'll raise the standards in every area of your life and business. There is only one real success: to live life on your terms, your own way.

I've set the stage. . . now it's up to you to execute.

P.S. There's a free gift for you near the end of this book in the Bonus Money Makers and Useful Resources section. This will skyrocket your profits. It's also a way to continue our relationship beyond this book. Please take a minute now to look at it and take action.

CHAPTER 1

AN ENTREPRENEUR'S WORST ADDICTION

WHETHER YOU'RE A MASTER OF SELF-DISCIPLINE OR STRUGGLING to break a bad habit, addiction affects all of us at some point in our lives. However, the addiction we'll discuss in this chapter isn't the run-of-the-mill caffeine or nicotine buzz; it's an addiction that becomes more and more prevalent in the entrepreneurial community with each passing year. It's one you may not even be aware of: information addiction.

A while back, I had a conversation with a colleague, and he mentioned he had read one hundred books on entrepreneurship within the course of a year. On the surface, this sounds like an impressive accomplishment. I know I certainly wouldn't have had the time to read that much. Yet when I asked him what those books helped him to accomplish, he was stumped. He couldn't provide me with a single instance of action he had taken after reading thousands of pages of entrepreneurial insight.

That's a big problem and one I often see among entrepreneurs. They consume, interact, post on social media, attend events, and then consume some more. The cycle just continues. Then, before they even realize it, a year has gone by, and they're in the same position that they were to begin with. They might know more, but their life hasn't changed.

Why is that? Why have we developed such an infatuation with information?

For starters, we're now exposed to it on a massive level. Moore's Law states that the amount of information doubles every two years.[1]

Here are a few key pieces of data that reveal just how much information we absorb on a daily basis.

Every minute:

- Facebook users share nearly 2.5 million pieces of content
- Twitter users tweet nearly 350,000 times
- Instagram users post nearly 500,000 new photos
- YouTube users upload seventy-two hours of new video content
- Apple users download nearly 75,000 apps
- Email users send over 200 million messages
- Amazon generates over $283,000 in online sales

According to IBM Marketing Cloud, 90 percent of the data in the world today was created in the last two years alone, with 2.5 quintillion bytes of data being created every single day.

Think about that for a second.

For every scroll, letter, book, poem, painting, photo, radio broadcast, movie, report, tape, CD, mp3, mp4, YouTube video, and social media post from the beginning of time until now, 90 percent of it was created in the last two years! With new devices, sensors, and technologies emerging, the data growth rate will only continue to accelerate.

There's also the accessibility factor. We have lightning-fast search engines and voice-activated technology ready to fuel our need for information at all times. According to ACI.com, Google received over 2 million search queries per minute in 2012—a number that has nearly doubled since. Today, Google receives over 4 million search queries per minute from the nearly three-billion-strong global internet population.[2] Based on those calculations, it's safe to say we likely won't see a decrease anytime soon.

---

1   Tardi, Carla. "Moore's Law Explained." Investopedia, Investopedia, 4 Mar. 2021, https://www.investopedia.com/terms/m/mooreslaw.asp.

2   "Google Search Statistics." Google Search Statistics - Internet Live Stats, www.internetlivestats.com/google-search-statistics

This age of information overload isn't just a trend or a temporary shift. It's our new norm. And while it might feel like an unbeatable battle, it's really just a matter of recognizing that information is simply just that: information. It's not action, nor execution, and constant consumption won't get you any closer to achieving your goals. If information was all you needed to become successful, we'd all be billionaires.

The problem I see with most entrepreneurs is they absorb so much information, whether by attending seminars, reading books, or listening to podcasts, they become overwhelmed. Then, they either take the wrong course of action or, worse, stay paralyzed. Don't let yourself fall into this vicious cycle! In order to achieve your goals, you must always remember:

Mastery is the highest form of accomplishment.

The only way to become successful is to master the fundamentals that match your end results and goals. **The immature learner wants to get as much information as they can as fast as they can, but you usually find them broke, stressed, and lacking real progress.** The mature person is very deliberate in what they study and put into their mind. Achievers focus on listening until they've fully digested and adopted the information into their daily lives.

If you're serious about becoming a true, World-Class entrepreneur, you must acknowledge the distractions that hold you back and harness your focus on correct execution. It's time to get addicted to results and outcomes, not information and knowledge. It's time to be more selective than you've ever been with what you consume. The results you achieve from previous information is the prerequisite for new consumption. You must have specific outcomes and criteria in mind when taking in anything new.

To get you started, below is a checklist of everything I consider before investing my time in new information. This has been a complete game-changer for my productivity, mindset, and results, and offers a simple solution to avoid unnecessary distractions or information overload. So, from now on, before you take on new information, ask yourself these questions:

☐ Is this information congruent to my ideal six-month vision? (We'll cover this in a later chapter)
☐ Is this information proven and taught by someone who has the results I want and has values similar to mine?
☐ Have I taken action on previous information I've learned?
☐ Am I certain this is the best information and training available on this subject?

The World-Class lifestyle demands you simplify your focus and get crystal clear on what you want and why. This is pivotal. I promise your "just one more" mentality is doing you no good. One more seminar, one more podcast, one more sales program, etc., is not what you need. You need to dial it in and truly master the principles discussed in this book. I'm going to give you a number of tools to do just that, but ultimately, you must be the one to take action. You must sell yourself on the exceptional life and work for it strategically because like most things in life, it won't just come to you—you have to create it.

ADDICTION MATH: CHECKING YOUR ROI

If you're someone who's spent tens of thousands of dollars on training, experiences, and knowledge you never use, you're definitely not alone. In fact, there are entire seminars, conferences, webinars, and training courses that focus on capturing people just like you: information junkies in search of their next high. I'll even go further and say universities are guilty of this as well. At a top-tier school, a four-year degree can cost more than two hundred thousand dollars when you include housing, food, and all other expenses. Yet, how many college graduates immediately focus on recouping that investment? Most people talk about college as an experience. They talk about the amazing people they met and how their minds were opened. And while that might be beneficial down the line and very valuable, experiences and friendships don't pay the bills. This is an area where universities are failing. They don't provide students with a solid path for recouping the investment they made in their education. If they did, they'd likely have a lot of uncomfortable questions to answer.

Every single decision you make from here on out should be with your eyes open and with a focus on getting a return on your investment. You can focus on experiences and adventures *after* you find your business success. That's part of the reward process. The next time you're ready to financially invest in another informational resource, ask yourself, "Will this piece of information make me more money than it costs?" The answer to this should also include associated costs.

Let's use attending an event as an example. Not only is there the cost of the ticket, but there's also your flight, hotel room, meals, cocktails, and most importantly, your time. If there's a financial benefit or opportunity at this event that recoups that cost, then great. It might be a safe bet. But if not, you may want to sit this one out. Don't let the fear of missing out or an addiction to information overrule your self-discipline. After all, there will always be another conference or seminar to attend. You must look at investments in informational resources as business decisions with a financial calculus, which will, in turn, allow your decision-making to mature.

If there's anything I want you to take away from this book, it's that building a World-Class life starts with making action-driven changes from within. In this case, that means making a conscious effort to step away from consumption. Consider how much new information you can take action on this year. Can you actually convert that knowledge into implementation, or will you be at the next training event before that knowledge reaches fruition? If you can change from emotion-centric to result-centric thinking, you'll become leaner and more efficient in how you build your life and business.

As for my colleague who read those one hundred books in a year, I challenged him to spend a portion of that time creating and producing instead of just consuming. One year later, he's created a successful investment coaching program and launched his first course. The information is important, but the execution of the right information is what separates professionals from amateurs.

It's time to get started on creating your Execution plan.

EXECUTION PLAN

What are some ways in which you could shift your focus from consumption to execution or from consumption to production?

_____
_____
_____
_____

Name the last three pieces of content you consumed in the previous thirty days. Examples: podcast, book, seminar, summit, video, etc.

1. _____
2. _____
3. _____

What tangible results have you seen from them?

_____
_____
_____
_____

What will your standard be for consuming new content?

_____
_____
_____
_____

What content from the previous six months created the biggest results for your life and business?

_____
_____
_____
_____
_____
_____

CHAPTER 2

THE SILENT KILLER

"People who grow up without a sense of how yesterday has affected today are
unlikely to have a strong sense of how today affects tomorrow."
—LYNNE CHENEY

IMAGINE THIS SCENARIO: YOU'RE STARVING, AND YOU WALK INTO A
room to find a cookie waiting for you. It's made perfectly, with just the
right balance of chewy and crumbly and melted chocolate chips. You're
told that you may eat this tasty cookie right now, or if you wait twenty
minutes, you may have two.

How would you react? Could you be patient and hold out for the
greater reward? Or do you think your neurochemistry would take over
and seize this opportunity to feed your hunger?

This concept is referred to as "instant pleasure" or "instant gratification" and has become one of the silent killers of many dreams and goals.
It's a terrible habit that many of us have been sucked into and involves
forgoing short-term pain that could potentially lead to long-term pleasure. Instead, we indulge in short-term pleasure that leads to long-term
pain. In other words, it's the process of avoiding what might provide
future benefit due to the lack of an instant reward.

The biggest problem with instant gratification is that it can often
lead to procrastination. So much, in fact, I even consider it a form of

self-sabotage, similar to that of addiction. In addition, people who get caught up in the instant pleasure trap still often expect results. They invest in a meager effort, blowing thousands of dollars in the process, then get frustrated when they don't see a return. I'm here to tell you it simply doesn't work that way! If we've learned anything about the historical course of entrepreneurship, it's that we take in what we put out. Why would anyone invest time in your product or service if you didn't invest the time yourself?

Many studies have been conducted about the impact instant gratification has on progress, but there's one in particular that stands out the most and is similar to the cookie scenario mentioned at the start of this chapter.

In 1960, a Stanford professor named Walter Mischel began conducting a series of important psychological studies that essentially changed how we view human desire. During his experiments, Mischel and his team brought hundreds of children into a room one by one, sat them down in a chair, and placed a marshmallow on a table in front of them. Then they were told the researcher would be leaving the room, and if they refrained from eating the marshmallow while the researcher was gone, they would be given another one upon his return.

So, the choice was simple: one treat right now or two treats later. In other words, small success now and no success later, or no success now and massive success later.

The researcher left the room for fifteen minutes. Some kids jumped up and ate the first marshmallow as soon as the researcher closed the door. Others wiggled, bounced, and scooted in their chairs as they tried to restrain themselves but eventually gave in to temptation a few minutes later. And finally, a few of the children managed to wait the entire time.

The interesting part came years later, as it usually does in success, and this is where the power of delayed gratification came to fruition. As the years rolled by and the children grew up, the researchers conducted extensive follow-up studies and tracked each child's progress in a number of areas. What they found was surprising: the children who were willing to delay gratification to receive the second marshmallow had higher SAT scores, lower levels of substance abuse, lower likelihood of obesity, better responses to stress, better social skills as reported by their parents, and generally better scores in a range of other life measures.

These experiments continued over the course of forty years, and the results were consistently the same. The groups who waited patiently for the second marshmallow succeeded far more often than the ones who didn't. This proves a simple truth that still rings true today: delaying gratification through self-discipline is critical for success in all facets of life.

Consider similar scenarios within your own life:

- If you delay the gratification of watching Netflix after a long day at your 9-to-5 and work on your side business, you'll be able to quit your job sooner.
- If you delay the gratification of buying junk food at the store, you'll eat healthier when you get home. In turn, you'll feel better about yourself.
- If you delay the gratification of skipping a workout or sleeping in and go for a run instead, you'll become stronger and more energized.
- If you delay the gratification of going out and partying until you've earned it, you'll avoid the stress of unfinished work.
- If you delay the gratification of buying nice things until you have the money, you'll appreciate your purchases more, knowing you genuinely earned them.

This may come easier for some than it does for others and often involves the way a person was raised. Going back to the marshmallow study, the question comes up as to why some children were capable of delaying gratification and others weren't. Despite what you may think, it wasn't just a matter of behavioral issues or personality traits, but rather, how familiar the children were with the future. Those who grew up in uneducated households seemed to have traits representative of "survival mode." In other words, they lived in the moment because that's all they had the capacity for. Whereas the children born into college-educated households were often more exposed to the concepts of goal setting and self-discipline, and therefore were able to utilize those practices on their own.

If you fall into the first category and grew up without much knowledge of self-discipline, that's likely impacted much of your progress in life. However, you must understand that your past DOES NOT dictate your future; your daily decisions do.

Don't use this study to justify your bad habits or deter your motivation. Instead, use it as a tool to better understand yourself and your daily decision-making. After all, the only way to permanently break a bad habit (like the need for instant gratification) is to first understand the root cause. If your parents didn't cause it, was it anxiety from something else? Could it be that you've been discouraged and you always find yourself looking for a quick fix? Whatever it may be, the most important takeaway is that you must start considering your future self in every decision you make.

HOW DO YOU BECOME BETTER AT DELAYING GRATIFICATION?

Delayed gratification is one of the most effective personality traits of successful people. Whether it be saving now to spend later, eating wisely for the sake of better health later, or sacrificing a little fun now to live an extraordinary life later, these examples and more prove that delayed gratification can have a tremendously positive impact on your life.

If you're someone who's struggling in this area, don't worry—you still have the capacity to change. Just like we train our muscles at the gym, we can train our brains to delay the need for gratification at any stage in life. Get started by trying some of the tactics below.

5 WAYS TO KILL THE INSTANT-PLEASURE TRAP

1. Clearly Define Your Goals

Weakness invades when our long-term goals are murky and hard to see, and instant gratification can overwhelm our desire to hit a goal when it is ill-defined. With clearly defined short- and long-term goals and the motivation required to reach them, you'll have a far easier time resisting instant pleasure.

If you're struggling to narrow down your goals into achievable steps, check out the World-Class Productivity Plan in Chapter 13 for step-by-step guidance.

2. Reward Yourself

Delaying gratification can be hard work, and it takes real willpower. Depending on what you want, it may take weeks, months, years, and sometimes even decades to achieve. However, breaking down your goals and rewarding yourself along the way can serve as a helpful reminder that delaying gratification leads you in the right direction. When choosing your reward, make sure it's not something that interferes with your progress. This applies to essentially any goal, business or personal. For example, if you're on a diet and reward yourself for working out by eating a cupcake, that essentially negates any potential progress from the workout. Focus on putting a healthy reward system in place, and you'll not only start to feel better about yourself, but you'll also be far less likely to seek out instant pleasure.

3. Align Yourself with Positive Influences

Are your friends and family helping or hurting your progress? This is a question many of us have to ask when pursuing a goal. If those you spend the most time with are focused on instant pleasure (drinking after work, unnecessary splurging, obsessing over social media, etc.) and fail to think about their future, then it might be time to cut ties. You wouldn't bring a recovering alcoholic into a bar, right? Then why surround yourself with people who fuel your temptations? Developing healthy relationships means finding individuals who share your ambition and drive, and in this case, desire for a brighter future.

4. Make the Hard Choices and Choose Growth in the Moment

We typically have two choices in life: the easy choice and the hard choice. It's natural to be drawn to the easy choice first; however, you'll find that continuously taking the easy way out makes life harder in the long run. You must actively train your brain to think critically before making a decision. Ask yourself the following:

- Is this the most intelligent choice I can make for my future?
- Will I be disappointed in myself for making this decision?
- Is this a decision my future self will thank me for?

The more often you do this, the quicker you'll learn to appreciate delayed gratification.

5. Visualize a Realistic Future

When we visualize our future selves, we often rely on unrealistic fantasies that require an overwhelming amount of change. This not only creates confusion about how to pursue a new path but also disappointment when the vision doesn't come to fruition. Instead of striving for the unreachable, try building your goals around a single event. Examples of this might include:

- Losing weight for an upcoming wedding
- Saving a certain amount of money for a future vacation
- Recording a specific number of episodes for a podcast launch

As important as it is to set realistic goals, it's equally important to visualize them using as much detail as possible. In fact, I recently had an experience with my brother in law that proves just how important the visualization process is. He was out of shape, sick of being tired all the time, and embarrassed by the state of his body. He was only willing to work out once a week and continued to make unhealthy lifestyle choices. My wife and I had a big event coming up that included most of our family, friends, and likely some pool time, and he was pretty uneasy about it. This is what I said to him:

"I want you to fast-forward to the big event we're having for your sister. Our entire family will be in town, and everybody will be at the pool. I want to think about how much better you'll feel about taking your shirt off. Imagine the compliments you'll get and how proud everyone will be with the progress you've made. Think of how much more confident you'll feel overall. The outcome for that day depends on the action you take now. Either you'll feel accomplished and proud, OR embarrassed and frustrated. Let that feeling drive your decisions from this point forward. Every time you don't feel like working out, fast-forward to that day. Don't just do it for your sister and family. Do it for yourself."

It's been eight months since we had that conversation, and he's lost thirty-five pounds so far. He now works out four to five times a week, makes health-conscious lifestyle choices, and has significantly cut back on the beer. (It's mainly because my wife is a wino and makes him drink wine instead). When you can fast-forward and get addicted to the feeling of future accomplishment instead of just living in the moment, you'll experience the true power of delayed gratification.

Like with many of the topics throughout this book, avoiding the instant gratification trap ultimately starts with self-awareness and a willingness to shift your perspective. When you can define what's important to you, you'll find it far easier to make choices that lead to true future fulfillment rather than just temporary happiness. People tend to express their distaste for change, but it becomes evident that people actually love change; what they hate is *transition*. When you learn to appreciate the transition, you'll look forward to the positive changes.

Is the instant gratification trap impacting your progress? Are there certain things sucking up too much time or energy in your life? Use the execution plan on the following page to start forming a solution.

EXECUTION PLAN

In this chapter, I gave you five ways to kill the instant-pleasure trap. Which one do you think would make the biggest impact on your future and why?

_____
_____
_____
_____

What are some decisions you can make now that your future self will thank you for six months from now?

_____
_____
_____
_____

What are some decisions you can make now that your future self and all those you care about will thank you for ten years from now?

_____
_____
_____
_____

When you think back on your life, where has instant pleasure hurt you the most?

_____
_____
_____
_____

What would some of the long-term consequences be if you continue to focus on instant pleasure versus delaying gratification?

_____

_____

_____

_____

What's one action you can take consistently every morning to help you set the tone for the day (i.e., making your bed, eating a healthy breakfast, working out, reviewing your goals, etc.)?

_____

_____

_____

_____

CHAPTER 3

THE NEW UNWRITTEN RULES FOR REAL SUCCESS AND FREEDOM

AS ENTREPRENEURS, GETTING REAL, SOLIDIFIED RESULTS IS OFTEN one of our main goals. We seek data to justify our investment in both business and life. This is one of the most appealing aspects of entrepreneurship: the adrenaline rush of watching a business grow, whether it be through climbing website traffic, engagement on social media, or a growing customer base.

However, through my years of working with successful entrepreneurs and even becoming one myself, the primary lesson I've learned is that logic or even financial prosperity doesn't always equate to real success. I've met top-dog entrepreneurs who've built multimillion-dollar businesses yet have completely unfulfilling lives. I've met influencers with millions of raving fans who struggle with long-term bouts of depression.

I used to naively think a Game Changer was someone who became the best in the world in their field and hit the peak of their profession, someone who changed an entire industry and made millions in the process. Yet, when I dove deep into the lives of society's so-called Game

Changers, I realized a lot of them gained notoriety by sacrificing in other areas of life that are more important in the long-term.

When we're at the end of our lives, facing death, our biggest regrets won't be that we didn't have more transactions, followers, or likes. They'll revolve around failed relationships, not having lived a fully authentic life, or wishing we had focused more time on things that really mattered. We'll wish we had created a legacy for our loved ones or took better care of the most important relationships in our lives.

While we all might define success differently, being a true Game Changer isn't just about success; it's about dedicating your life to something that's bigger than yourself and doing so in a World-Class way. The greatest contribution you can make to the world is to become the best version of yourself while creating an amazing lifestyle that you're proud of. You don't need to make millions to be World-Class, and you don't need millions of followers to become a Game Changer or to feel worthy. However, you do need to execute in a few areas that many people take for granted, and that means giving yourself some special attention.

Society has become obsessed with watching others. From gawking at someone's daily life on reality television to idolizing star athletes to following flashy entrepreneurs on social media, we have developed an unappeasable appetite for watching others do and become something.

Although watching those around us is not all bad, we need to ask ourselves, "What am *I* doing to become someone special?" This doesn't mean you need to set your goals on becoming the next star athlete, business celebrity, or billionaire. It's simpler than that. Instead, how about aspiring to become the best possible version of yourself? How about shifting your perspective and ambition away from the limelight and toward something more fulfilling, like bettering your best and seeing what you're truly capable of?

Becoming the best possible version of yourself will be unique for everyone; there's no exact definition of what it is. However, after studying, interviewing, and being mentored by dozens of people I personally consider to be World-Class, I've identified a number of unwritten laws by which they all abide. If you want to become World-Class, you need to follow these rules.

THE EIGHT RULES OF WORLD-CLASS PEOPLE

The actual definition of a Game Changer is "a newly introduced element or factor that changes an existing situation or activity in a significant way." In this specific context there are multiple aspects of becoming a Game Changer, and those operating at the World-Class level have a lot of similarities. Now, I know many of you who are reading this are likely itching to get into the strategy and business side of the book, and I promise it's coming soon. But it's of vital importance that we first establish the foundation of what it truly means to be a World-Class human so that you can start the internal transition on your own.

RULE 1: ALWAYS DO THE RIGHT THING

While this might sound near impossible, you'd be surprised at how instinctual it becomes when you put it into frequent practice. Start by making a conscious effort to put integrity above all else. This means no scheming, no lying, no exaggerating, and owning up to your faults. Your personal values should be the ultimate driver of how you run your business.

> **It's not about who's right; it's about what's right.**

I've personally found that being open and honest about a mistake I've made not only removes internal stress but also has a more positive outcome in the end, whether it's gaining more trust with colleagues or protecting my reputation. It's the full circle of good karma: when you put good in, you'll get it back.

RULE 2: LIVE BY YOUR STANDARDS, PRINCIPLES, AND VALUES

Specifically, don't let your values waiver based on your environment or who you associate with. You might find yourself wanting to put on a front when around materialistic people, but you'll gain far more respect by being your unique self at all times. You must base everything on your principles and values without letting emotions or fear get in the way. This is an important part of long-term happiness and peace of mind.

Your self-worth is built when you respect your authentic self regardless of circumstance or environment.

RULE 3: VALUE YOUR WORD ABOVE ALL ELSE

Reliability is a precious commodity in this day and age, and World-Class people understand that. No one is perfect, and there might be times when you fail to follow through, but it's important to take 100 percent responsibility for it, provide a legitimate reason for your lack of follow-through, and make an effort to regain trust. Integrity should always be at the top of your priority list. You can't recover your words after they've been said, so the weight you place on each one is extremely powerful. I try my very best to live by these six words always: *Think it through, then follow through.*

RULE 4: DON'T JUDGE OTHERS, BUT RATHER ACCEPT AND APPRECIATE

The effect you have on others is one of your most valuable currencies and is a major component in becoming World-Class. You must treat every person you come into contact with like they are the most important person in the world because ultimately, they are. You'll also find that making positive judgments about people rather than negative ones will boost your confidence and your self-worth. While this may not come naturally for some, you must continuously strive to negate your ego and push judgment-fueled insecurities aside. In doing so, you'll find that people are never as simple as we tend to view them. Judge less, observe more, and embrace unique perspectives.

RULE 5: FOCUS ON EMOTIONAL MATURITY

There are two options when it comes to how we handle our emotions: we control them, or they control us. Those operating at World-Class levels always stay in control of their emotions, whether through practiced self-reflection or emotional-management strategies. You must learn how to recognize your highs and lows and avoid swinging too far to either side. Believe me, nothing will make a bigger difference in your attitude, energy, consistency, and bank account than this rule. I was forced to learn the importance of emotional IQ at an early stage of my business after massive failure. I realized that most decisions derived from a place of emotion are usually the wrong ones. All great achievers and those living World-Class lives use logic and intelligence in every decision they make. You'll see your influence, income, and results sky-rocket when you do the same.

RULE 6: LEAVE OTHERS BETTER THAN YOU FOUND THEM

While entrepreneurship can often feel like an isolating endeavor, it's crucial to stay focused on helping others in everything you do. By putting your efforts toward generosity and giving back, you'll not only experience benefits within your business but in your life as well. This doesn't mean just donate to a charity—I'm talking about creating a direct, positive impact on everyone you come into contact with. Make it a habit to leave people in a better state than you found them; happier, healthier, stronger, and wealthier. Build them up, make them feel exceptional, and never tear them down. This is a major factor in being an exceptional, World-Class person, and will come back in the same way as doing the right thing, through the circle of good karma.

RULE 7: BE EXTREMELY AUTHENTIC AND GENUINE

Being your authentic self can feel risky in our now social media-obsessed world. We just try to fit in, be liked, and be accepted by other human beings. As a result, the images we present have become mere representations of who we *think* we should be and not reflections of who we really are. World-Class people never try to be someone they're not; they commit to everything they say and do. And while authenticity isn't exactly a major focus in our social media-driven culture, it can be one of the most powerful drivers in creating positive relationships and building trust. It takes a lot of energy to try and be someone you're not, and it often kills self-worth over time. Don't let your actions or words be influenced by the opinions of others. Instead, focus on discovering your unique qualities and perspectives and share them with pride.

RULE 8: PROTECT YOUR REPUTATION

You may not be able to prevent jealous or insecure people from their attempts to tarnish your name, but you can build a solid enough reputation that lies told by others will be revealed for what they are: idiotic and false. I've learned through the years that reputation always exceeds money. It can take thirty years to build, and just thirty seconds of bad judgment can tear it down. However, by actively practicing the rules listed above, your good reputation will develop hand in hand.

You don't need to become the next Elon Musk or create the next billion-dollar idea. While there's nothing wrong with having ambition or striving for greatness, you must also take some of the energy that you've invested in your business and invest it in your life. First, focus on becoming a Game Changer for your family, your city, and your company. THEN focus on the rest.

I'm not interested in helping people who want to retire at thirty, live on a beach, and do nothing, or those who simply dabble in entrepreneurship. There are enough of those people already. I'm interested in helping the individuals who are striving to build a legacy focused around their values, those who truly want to create something bigger than themselves. I'm interested in the people who want to solve huge problems in their marketplace. We all have a bigger purpose than the lives we're currently living, and it's my hope that this book is the wake-up call our generation desperately needs.

How do you plan to become a World-Class human being? Use the execution plan on the following page to write out your thoughts.

EXECUTION PLAN

In what area of life are you currently falling behind right now?

_____
_____
_____

In what areas do you want to become more World-Class?

_____
_____
_____

Have you ever gone against what was popular to stay true to your values? If so, when?

_____
_____
_____

How did it make you feel?

_____
_____
_____

Who you respect is who you become. Who are your top five role models and people you respect?

1. _____
2. _____
3. _____
4. _____
5. _____

What similar qualities does each of these individuals have?

_____

_____

_____

What do you want your life to be like five years from now?

_____

_____

_____

For example, what is the condition of your body? How are your relationships with friends, family, and loved ones? What is your financial situation? Write out a one-page summary of your answer below, and try to focus on as many different aspects of your future reality as possible.

_____

_____

_____

_____

_____

_____

_____

_____

_____

_____

_____

_____

_____

_____

_____

_____

_____

_____

_____

_____

_____

CHAPTER 4

RULE 1

WORLD-CLASS SELF-AWARENESS

THE PERSPECTIVE SHIFT

> **What you don't know about yourself controls your life.**

Have you ever been in a situation where your immediate reaction surprised you?

Maybe a loved one got a promotion, and rather than feeling excited for them, you felt jealous and responded in a cold, negative way. Or maybe a friend confronted you about a mistake you made, and rather than accepting responsibility, you exploded and denied any wrongdoing.

Scenarios like these are not uncommon for human beings. We're complex creatures with a lot of moving parts to control, many of which were formed by our own personal experiences, fears, beliefs, thoughts, and so forth.

So, how do we get better at controlling these pieces?

Through active self-awareness.

WHAT IS SELF-AWARENESS?

While the concept itself sounds fairly obvious, self-awareness is more than just being aware of oneself. It's the process of focusing awareness internally, of being aware of your feelings, thoughts, habits, physical sensations, and reactions. Think back to a time when you used a "gut feeling" or "instinct" to make a decision. It likely felt uncomfortable in the moment, but you also knew deep down it was the right choice, whether based on past experiences or just understanding your own personal needs. That decision-making process is the essence of self-awareness.

In transitioning to the World-Class life, you'll be making a lot of tough choices that will inevitably impact your future, and utilizing self-awareness could mean the difference between living a life on your terms or one of massive regret. What we don't know about ourselves limits our ability to connect with others and can even delay our desire to move forward.

If we aren't aware of a specific fear, we can't make the choice to conquer that fear.

If we aren't aware of a negative emotion that limits our productivity, we aren't able to eradicate it.

If we don't force ourselves to think differently, we'll continue to make the same mistakes again and again.

If we don't know which stories we play in our minds don't serve us, we'll never know which ones to recreate.

Ultimately, we can only make conscious choices about the things we are conscious of.

This isn't something you'll find in an investment book or hear about on an entrepreneurial podcast because nearly all business-strategy sources rely on the perspective of the teacher. That doesn't necessarily mean it lacks value, but by consuming the thoughts and ideas of others, you essentially drown out your own inner voice.

For most of our lives, our surroundings, our environment, and societal expectations have forced us out of being ourselves. They've forced us to think a certain way and forced us to try and fit in with everybody else. Thinking for yourself has become a rare commodity, and independent thinkers have a big advantage over those who don't. The power is in the ability to not be influenced by the things that don't serve us. The only time others can affect you is if you haven't taken the time to know yourself at a deeper level.

This is why I've spent the past couple of years putting myself at the top of my priority list. I'm getting to know myself inside and out, so I can better understand my decision-making, reactions, and the steps I need to take to continue thriving. Putting yourself first isn't selfish; it's necessary. In fact, over the course of the last year, I have:

- Read the least number of books that I have in ten years
- Attended zero seminars
- Listened to one podcast
- Had one mentor
- Invested in one proven program as opposed to three or four

On the surface, it might seem like I've taken a step back on gaining knowledge, but that's not the case. I've simply shifted my attention to self-awareness and relying on what I already know, as well as on the network I've built to make decisions for my business. In doing so, I've seen more growth in my bottom-line results. The number of people our brand is reaching has increased, as well as the number of paid speaking engagements. Opportunities are coming my way more than ever before. When you start to focus on your self-awareness, the decisions you make become exclusively beneficial for you and, therefore, become more effective in your life and business.

THE BENEFITS OF SELF-AWARENESS

Self-awareness is a concept interwoven within many of the philosophies that make up our moral infrastructure, mainly because Greek philosophers believed that self-knowledge was the highest form of knowledge. They also claimed it was the hardest to master. The Greek philosopher Thales claimed that to know thyself is the "most difficult thing to do," whereas the easiest thing is to "give others advice." This theory directly explains why we have so many self-proclaimed gurus offering up their opinions on anything and everything; they're able to make money doing something that requires little effort, that essentially anyone could do.

The real question is, how many of those gurus actually follow their own advice? To take it further, how many of those gurus are actually living World-Class lives?

In learning to listen and reflect on your own internal feelings, you'll not only have better control over your emotions; you'll be able to create your own individualized framework for success.

A FEW OTHER KEY BENEFITS

Enriched emotional intelligence and greater empathy and listening skills

Going back to what we discussed in the previous chapter, the ability to listen to others and empathize with them is a major component in gaining trust and becoming likable among your peers. If people enjoy working with you, you'll inevitably receive more opportunities.

Improved critical-thinking skills and decision-making

Wouldn't it be nice to feel completely confident in the decisions you make? This is where self-reflection comes in handy. Learning how to evaluate your own thoughts and feelings requires using a part of the brain that most of us avoid using, as it's also where we house our emotional baggage. However, by confronting that baggage and learning to think beyond self-perceived limitations, you're polishing critical thinking skills that can be used to make strategic, well-thought-out decisions. It becomes easier to make the right decisions when you determine what your real values are.

Enhanced leadership capabilities and capacity

Even if you don't consider yourself a leader, having the qualities of a leader is a key factor in personal and financial growth. This doesn't necessarily mean that you have to lead a team, but you must be able to stand firm in your decisions and capabilities to reach the level of World-Class. It's important to never let your emotions overpower your intelligence.

When it comes down to it, knowing yourself inside and out gives you a competitive edge in both business and life. It requires less emotional energy than trying to fit in or please others, which makes for a much easier climb to the top. In fact, I recently had an experience at an event that reminded me just how valuable self-awareness can be.

I was set to give a speech at Success Live, one of the biggest events of the year for entrepreneurs, and would be doing so in front of a crowd of about 3,500. As I sat in the hotel lobby, eating my breakfast, I began to notice the speakers walking into the event space. They were all dressed to the nines. I'm talking collared shirts, full suits, ties, the whole nine yards. I remember Les Brown walking by in a full three-piece suit. Whereas I, the youngest speaker at the event, was sporting jeans and an Oregon Boy hat. Before you judge, I want you to know I was giving a talk about "the power of knowing yourself, and how to thrive in the NEW ECONOMY." The new economy allows for people to be themselves and still thrive. I wore a suit for seven years while building my direct sales company, and at the time of this event, I preferred to be myself versus fitting in.

I immediately began to second-guess my wardrobe choice and found myself drowning in a flood of anxious thoughts.

Will being dressed this casually make me stand out in a negative way?

Will the audience take me seriously?

Will the other speakers take me seriously?

Will I go down in history as the only speaker who didn't bring a personal stylist to this event?

After a few minutes of panic, I snapped myself out of it and started to realize that dwelling on something so insignificant was not only a waste of my focus but also didn't define me as an individual. I was dressed casually because I was representing myself authentically, which was why I had been booked in the first place! I didn't gain an audience by being yet another speaker in a suit, and my clothing choice had nothing to do with the value I brought to the table. After coming to that conclusion, I felt far more in control of my nerves, was able to turn my insecurity into confidence, and ended up giving one of the best speeches of my career—one that has gotten me booked for other events and significantly expanded my audience reach overall. (You can watch this speech on my YouTube channel).

Thinking back on it now, I realize had I not been able to focus on my self-awareness and drown out those annoying voices of self-doubt, the outcome of that day could have been far different. I probably would have been a sweaty, nervous wreck of a speaker who was focused more on the thoughts of the audience than on my own speech, which could have resulted in mistakes, embarrassment, and a damaged reputation.

And that right there is the value of self-awareness.

Self-awareness keeps us grounded when we start questioning our decisions and removes the constant need to compare and evaluate ourselves using the standards of others, whether it be clothing choices, job title, the type of car we drive, and so forth. The precious time we spend trying to identify and follow the trends of society could be better used to set trends ourselves, which we're all fully capable of. It's the ones who truly understand themselves inside and out that set trends; those who are living a World-Class and purposeful life. Being the version of you that others have created is not your responsibility. Being yourself is.

THE SELF-AWARENESS ASSESSMENT

As instinctual as it sounds, self-awareness is actually one of the hardest traits for humans to master, mainly due to the fact that we spend most of our lives living in a state of autopilot. We often rely on our routines, habits, and reactions to get by. This isn't necessarily a bad thing; if we stopped and thought about every single action we took, we'd never get anything done. However, the problem arises when we remain on autopilot for so long that we forget we're on autopilot altogether.

To truly understand yourself, you have to be willing to give yourself special attention and understand that gaining ultimate power is about knowing your strengths and weaknesses. It's about having a clear understanding of your motives and recognizing when it's necessary to stop and reflect. In doing so, you'll train your brain to do this instinctively, resulting in better decision-making, less stress, and more confidence overall.

To get you started, I've prepared a set of self-reflective questions below. These questions are specifically designed to help you gain clarity as to who you are at the deepest level and reveal any personal thoughts or emotions that you may have been blocking out. I encourage you to take your time with this exercise and be as intentional as possible with your answers. Don't think about your kids, your job, your spouse, or anything else that might steal your focus. This is YOU time. Embrace it.

1. What would you say are your top three values?

    1. _____

    2. _____

    3. _____

2. What three character traits or values do you want to be included in your eulogy to describe you?

    1. _____

    2. _____

    3. _____

3. In just three words, what is your philosophy for living?

    1. _____

    2. _____

    3. _____

4. What three core values do you want to pass on to your children and grandchildren?

    1. _____

    2. _____

    3. _____

5. What are the top three qualities of your ideal business partner?

    1. _____

    2. _____

    3. _____

6. What are the top three qualities of your ideal life partner?

    1. _____

    2. _____

    3. _____

7. Imagine your dream day. What three emotions or values describe your experience?

    1. _____

    2. _____

    3. _____

8. What three core values do you want people to think of when they think of your business?

    1. _____

    2. _____

    3. _____

9. Take a few minutes and make a list of all the things you do well. What do you have the most experience in? List the things you're passionate about and love to spend time doing; the things that have yielded results. If you have trouble coming up with them, think about what you're drawn to when you procrastinate or what you think about while daydreaming.

    _____

    _____

    _____

    _____

10. What do you usually enjoy doing without being asked? What must you be dragged away from doing? What do you focus on most enthusiastically?

    _____

    _____

    _____

    _____

11. What are your talents? Is there anything that comes as second nature to you? List all the things you seem to be naturally good at.

    _____

    _____

    _____

    _____

    _____

12. What are your top five strengths?

     1. _____

     2. _____

     3. _____

     4. _____

     5. _____

13. What do you think your best skills are?

_____

_____

_____

_____

_____

14. List some ways you could enhance those skills.

_____

_____

_____

_____

_____

15. What is one thing that makes you special and unique? Don't focus on what you aren't, what you wish to be, or what others might expect from you.

_____

_____

_____

_____

_____

_____

GATHERING VALUED OPINIONS

Some of the best advice I ever received was to "take few opinions," but in this case, it's important to gather valued opinions. While self-awareness is primarily about our own internal perception, getting outside perspectives from those we trust and respect can help create a fuller picture.

This is what we'll focus on in this next section. By the end of this chapter, you'll not only have a greater understanding of how you see yourself, but you'll also be able to compare each assessment and determine if there are any major differences. The end goal is for each assessment to be as similar as possible because it will show that you are being your authentic self at all times.

In my last book, *6 Months to 6 Figures*, I included a pre-written email that readers could use to find out more about their unique abilities, and I got such an overwhelmingly positive response I decided to include an updated version here as well. I want you to send this email to the top ten people you spend the most time with—those who truly know you inside and out and whose opinion you value.

THE EMAIL TEMPLATE

Hey _____,

Thanks in advance for taking this email seriously! I genuinely appreciate your time, and I know how valuable it is. I'm only sending this email to the ten most influential people in my life—the people I respect and who raise my standards and challenge my thinking. I'm going through a demanding book about the concept of our unique abilities. I really want to get outside perspectives from others to find out where I might excel. I'm NOT doing this for my ego or to fish for compliments, but simply to see how I can best serve. I want to know myself at a deeper level and create greater clarity for my future. Not just for myself, but for my family and for those I care about, so once again, thank you for your honest feedback.

I'd really appreciate your feedback as to what you feel my unique abilities are.

Your response can include a list of my talents and abilities, characteristics that describe me, what I'm good at, how you think I do things, what you count on me for, and any other distinguishing features you see about who I am. Don't hold back, either :)

If you're interested in helping me, I would be grateful if you could respond within the next seven days. Thanks for your support, and I really look forward to hearing your feedback!

Thanks again,
[your name]

Which ten people will you send this email to?

1. _____
2. _____
3. _____
4. _____
5. _____
6. _____
7. _____
8. _____
9. _____
10. _____

Once you've received your responses, jot down a summary of them below. What did you learn about yourself? What did your recipients say was your greatest strengths? Did they mention anything that makes you unique?

_____
_____
_____
_____
_____

Were there any answers that genuinely surprised you?

_____
_____
_____

Which responses seemed the most obvious?

_____
_____
_____

What did you disagree with?

_____

_____

_____

Were there any common themes among all of the responses?

_____

_____

_____

DIGGING DEEPER

In this next section, we'll connect your values with your strengths, passions, and results.

Name five people who have similar values and the lifestyle and results you desire. Spend some time thinking about who you follow the most, why you follow them, and what attracts you to these specific people and their professions.

Person 1

Who is it? _____

What do they do? _____

Why do you respect them? _____

_____

Person 2

Who is it? _____

What do they do? _____

Why do you respect them? _____

_____

Person 3

Who is it? _____

What do they do? _____

Why do you respect them? _____

_____

Person 4

Who is it? _____

What do they do? _____

Why do you respect them? _____

_____

Person 5

Who is it? _____

What do they do? _____

Why do you respect them? _____

_____

Now, cross-reference the similarities. Do they match your strengths and unique abilities?

_____

_____

_____

WHAT'S NEXT?

Congrats! You've now completed the full assessment and should have a much better understanding of who you are at your deepest level. I encourage you to refer back to this assessment when you feel insecure or doubt your capabilities. In doing so, you'll train your brain to automatically reflect and focus on internal self-awareness during challenging situations.

Remember, your ideal life won't just show up; it must be purposely created. Don't sell yourself short or let those annoying voices of self-doubt get in the way. Embrace your uniqueness, course-correct when needed, and most importantly, never stop reflecting.

Looking for more reflection practice? Use the execution plan on the following page to reflect on what you've learned throughout this chapter.

EXECUTION PLAN

What were your biggest realizations from this chapter?

_____

_____

_____

On a scale of 1–10, how well would you say you truly know yourself, with 1 being not at all and 10 being a master?

   1   2   3   4   5   6   7   8   9   10

What actions can you take to help get your score closer to a 10?

_____

_____

_____

What would have the biggest impact on your long-term success if implemented into your daily life?

_____

_____

_____

If you continue to let others affect your standards, your confidence, and your decisions, what would it cost you in the long-term?

_____

_____

_____

What is the first action you will take after reading this chapter?

_____

RULE 2

WORLD-CLASS CIRCLE OF GENIUS AND RELATIONSHIPS

BUILDING A MILLION DOLLAR NETWORK

> The only things that will really change your life are the people you meet and the connections you develop along the way.

As you journey into creating a World-Class life, you'll meet many individuals who will either hurt or help your progress. Some will prove to be excellent resources, such as mentors who offer game-changing advice or friends who hold you accountable when you start to veer off course. Others will do everything within their power to prevent you from succeeding. That's the game of networking, and if you learn how to play it right, it could be one of the most valuable contributors to your success. Nobody is strong enough to overcome the power of association, which is why elevating your circle of influence is so important.

My first real experience with networking came back in 2008. I was struggling with my direct sales business and couldn't figure out why. I worked fifty hours a week without seeing any real results or progress, and everyone I spoke to kept giving me the exact same advice: if you work harder, progress will come. So, I raised my weekly hours to sixty, then eighty, and after months of overworking myself, I realized maybe the advice I received wasn't the advice I should be following. I then decided to seek out a mentor who was able to offer me direct, personal support, and that completely changed the way I viewed productivity.

By the end of 2008, I had streamlined my entire system. In 2009, I ended up being the youngest (and fastest) manager in my company's sixty-year history to reach $1 million in annual sales. The following year, we grew even bigger. However, through this unexpected growth, I also became cocky and arrogant. I was completely convinced I knew all of the "secrets" and that a mentor couldn't offer me any more value than I could offer myself. As a result, I dropped my mentor, lost my circle of influence, and then just like that, my business results began to plummet. I then had to spend the entirety of 2012 just trying to keep my business afloat.

This still remains one of the biggest and most expensive mistakes I've made in my career, but it taught me the immense value of having the right network and a wise mentor.

HERE ARE A FEW KEY TAKEAWAYS I LEARNED FROM THIS EXPERIENCE

Building valuable relationships with successful individuals shifts your perspective and opens up a whole new world, a new way of thinking, and a brand new you.

When you associate with millionaires or people who simply play the game at a higher level than you, these powerful individuals teach you the importance of having high standards for yourself and for those around you. Immersing yourself in this type of environment helps you to grow and succeed at an accelerated rate.

A smart person learns from their mistakes, as all successful people do, but those wanting World-Class results also learn from *others'* mistakes, so they don't waste time repeating them. This can cut your learning curve in half.

A powerful network enables you to play the game of life on your own terms. This will drastically help to accelerate your business while instantaneously increasing your value to your company and the marketplace.

One of the biggest breakthroughs and perspective shifts of my life occurred as a result of building my network. I used to bang my head against the wall when I didn't know the answer to a specific business question or when I lacked clarity on my next steps. This caused me a lot of stress, anxiety, and wasted time when I first started out, but once I started building my network strategically, I realized I no longer needed to have the answers to all of my business problems. My network did. I no longer needed to "figure everything out" on my own because my network had likely been where I wanted to go, and they could guide me. I'm now only one phone call away from solving any business problem.

> **When you have the right network, you don't need to figure everything out yourself.**

GIVERS, TAKERS, AND MATCHERS

I want to bring you a fresh perspective and a new way of looking at networking—one that's been proven to work in the new economy.

In the book *Give and Take*, Adam Grant argues that people fall into one of three categories: givers, takers, and matchers. In a nutshell, givers are motivated to take care of others, takers are primarily motivated by self-interest, and matchers typically give to others with the expectation of getting something back.

It's important to understand which category you fit into, as that will give you a foundation for how to pursue networking moving forward. Let's delve a little deeper into the characteristics of each category:

COMMON CHARACTERISTICS OF GIVERS
(THE RAREST OF THE THREE)

- Tilt reciprocity in the other direction, preferring to give more than they get

- Less focused on themselves; more focused on the needs of others
- Continuously strive to give in every way possible, whether it's by sharing time, energy, knowledge, ideas, or connections

COMMON CHARACTERISTICS OF TAKERS

- They like to get more than they give
- They tilt reciprocity in their own favor, putting their own interests ahead of others' needs
- They believe that the world is a competitive, dog-eat-dog place
- They feel that in order to succeed, they must be better than others
- To prove their competence, they self-promote and make sure they get plenty of credit for their efforts
- They're not necessarily cruel or cutthroat; they're just cautious and self-protective (They think, if I don't look out for myself, no one else will)

Citing Yale Psychologist Margaret Clark's research, Grant argues that outside of the workplace, most of us are givers when it comes to close relationships like marriages and friendships. We contribute without preoccupation or a need to keep score. In the workplace, however, few of us are pure givers or takers. Rather, we typically fall under the third style: matchers.

COMMON CHARACTERISTICS OF MATCHERS

- They strive to preserve an equal balance of giving and getting
- They operate on the principles of fairness
- They protect themselves by seeking reciprocity
- Their relationships are often governed by an exchange of favors

Giving, taking, and matching are three fundamental styles of social interaction, but the lines between them aren't hard and fast. You might find you shift from one reciprocity style to another as you navigate different work roles and relationships. For example, you may act like a taker when negotiating your salary, a giver when mentoring someone with less experience, and a matcher when sharing expertise with a colleague.

However, evidence shows the vast majority of people primarily develop a reciprocal style at work, which also captures how they approach networking. And this primary style can play just as much of a role in our success as hard work, talent, and luck.

The most successful networkers and relationship builders I know are givers. They always look to add value, solve problems, and make life easier for others without expecting anything in return. And believe it or not, it usually comes back to them tenfold. Does it occasionally backfire? Of course, but it's all about being strategic about who receives the end value.

Networking is a broad concept with many different variables, but if you know the source behind your motives, you'll have a far easier time implementing strategy into your social interactions. So, with that, let's delve deeper into the dos and don'ts of successful networking.

NETWORKING MISTAKES TO AVOID

Through my fifteen years of being an entrepreneur, I've learned there are a lot of different ways to make connections with colleagues, though very few resources actually teach you how. Everyone has different preferences, contact methods, platforms, and so forth, so how do you know which methods work and which ones to avoid?

I've had to rely on the trial-and-error method, which has been costly and frustrating at times, but it's also helped me develop a solid understanding of which strategies are most effective and which ones result in little to no return. A few examples of networking mistakes include:

- Reaching out with no strategy
- Reaching out once and never following up
- Only reaching out on one platform
- Not having a proven approach

These mistakes won't necessarily hurt your career, though they will prove to be counterproductive and could cause years of regret and frustration. Trust me, I've been there.

On the other hand, there are mistakes that will absolutely impact your career, and you must avoid them at all costs.

1. LACKING A NETWORKING STANDARD

The strategy and intention behind networking often determines its effectiveness. Make sure you're reaching out to the right people: those who have the results you want, and have similar values. For example, if family is your number-one value, then having a flexible schedule is a necessity. Therefore, you don't want to waste your efforts connecting with someone who works eighty hours a week and has meetings until 11 p.m. I'm not saying it's a bad strategy to connect; it's simply incongruent with your values and lifestyle, so any guidance they offer likely wouldn't align with your needs. You become who you respect, so it's important to be strategic and make sure you research who you reaching out to. Our Game Changers Academy has been interviewing elite entrepreneurs, world leaders, entertainers, and athletes since 2012. It's very important for us to have standards for who we book, as it protects and reflects our culture. If I promote being World-Class in life and business, but we have a speaker who doesn't make time for his family or values money over family, then it's incongruent to our culture.

2. ASKING FOR THEIR TIME RIGHT AWAY

I consider this one a networking crime, and I'm often shocked by how frequently it occurs. The fact of the matter is, time is the most valuable commodity on earth, especially for those in a high-income bracket and in high-demand. They know any time spent is money potentially made or wasted, so in general, they aren't willing to spare it unless there's something in it for them. By immediately asking for someone's time without having anything to offer in return, you make a very predictable mistake that's reflective of a rookie. It could even convey a sense of entitlement and lack of self-awareness as if you're suggesting they owe you something despite the difference in your career levels.

I made this mistake frequently in my early years, and generally, it never turned out the way I wanted. Now that I'm on the other side of the success spectrum and have people reaching out to me, I definitely understand why it didn't. There are simply too many requests to be able to appease everyone, and they all sound the same.

This is also why it's important to reach out in a creative, intentional way. By taking that extra step, you not only separate yourself from the pack, but you also show the recipient that you're willing to put in the effort for their time or attention.

A perfect example of this is a handwritten letter I recently received from a sixteen-year-old Canadian girl who wanted me to take part in a summit she put together. She started the letter with a personalized approach, talking about how much she loved my book, stating she had reviewed and promoted it all over her social media. She then dove deep into the "why" behind what she was doing, which was written in such a genuine, touching way. I felt an emotional connection to her before I even got to her request. Needless to say, she got my attention, and I'm now scheduled to speak at her summit later this year.

So how did a sixteen-year-old cut through all the noise and get me to commit to a summit when I had turned down over a hundred podcasts and summit invitations in just the last six months alone?

Simple:

- She took a different approach by mailing a handwritten invitation
- She showed she was serious by taking action before asking for anything
- She shared the "why" and got me emotionally involved
- She followed up with me on multiple platforms

This combination, mixed with the right approach, will drastically increase the chances of getting a response from the people you reach out to.

THE PROVEN THREE-STEP SYSTEM TO BUILDING YOUR MILLION DOLLAR NETWORK AND GETTING AHOLD OF ANYONE IN THE NEW DIGITAL ERA

The key to successful networking is understanding there is no one-size-fits-all method. However, by taking a logical, strategic approach, you can improve the chances of making it worth your effort. As I've stated before, it's important to align your networking with your values, priorities, and future vision, as failing to do so can result in a lot of wasted effort. It can also be helpful to plan your connections in advance to pinpoint the potential value they might offer.

I rely on a very simple three-step approach for this as it helps me to clearly think through the purpose of my outreach. I've included each step below, as well as a place to jot down your answers. Give it a shot:

STEP 1: CREATE YOUR DREAM TEN LIST

Write down the names of ten individuals and the reasons why you'd like to connect with them. Consider their strengths, what they specialize in, and the specific purposes they serve.

Here are the ten categories I typically use when creating my lists:

- Paid mentorship
- Quick advice or guidance
- Book endorsement or testimonial
- Financial investment in your startup/product
- Asking them to speak at your event/summit/academy
- Introduce them to another person you feel they could do business with
- Sharing an opportunity
- Expressing gratitude
- Cross-promotion
- Potential partnership

Find the similarities

How can you be sure these individuals are fully aligned with your vision? Use a cross-referencing approach by jotting down any similarities you have. A few examples might include:

- Same industry
- Similar mission

- Similar lifestyle
- Same religious or political views

Define the end goal

What's the ideal outcome for reaching out to each of these individuals? Even if it seems unrealistic, make a note of it. This will ensure you remain focused on their core values throughout the development of your relationship. Here are some examples of outcomes:

- They introduce you to their circle of influence
- They teach you how to scale your business
- They help you get a speaking engagement
- They're a guest on your podcast
- They collaborate with you on a project
- You interview them for your show

Now it's your turn! Put the three steps above into action by creating your own connection list.

PERSON 1

Name: _____

Main similarity: _____

Ideal end goal: _____

PERSON 2

Name: _____

Main similarity: _____

Ideal end goal: _____

PERSON 3

Name: _____

Main similarity: _____

Ideal end goal: _____

PERSON 4

    Name: _____

    Main similarity: _____

    Ideal end goal: _____

PERSON 5

    Name: _____

    Main similarity: _____

    Ideal end goal: _____

PERSON 6

    Name: _____

    Main similarity: _____

    Ideal end goal: _____

PERSON 7

    Name: _____

    Main similarity: _____

    Ideal end goal: _____

PERSON 8

    Name: _____

    Main similarity: _____

    Ideal end goal: _____

PERSON 9

    Name: _____

    Main similarity: _____

    Ideal end goal: _____

PERSON 10

    Name: _____

    Main similarity: _____

    Ideal end goal: _____

It's most important to remember you must be patient throughout this process. Developing a relationship with someone doesn't happen overnight, and it can take time to establish your ideal outcomes and visions. However, once you start to crystalize who you need to follow, connect with, and study, it becomes far easier to make that initial leap. You can systemize a lot of things, but you can't systemize building genuine relationships.

STEP 2. TAKE ACTION AND ADD VALUE FIRST

Everybody's favorite radio station is WIIFM, which stands for "What's in it for me?" If the most common networking styles are takers and matchers, then why not set yourself apart as a giver? This is one of the most important game-changing strategies of networking, yet it's also the least utilized. In fact, my friend and former VP of the LA Clippers, Kevin Eastman, previously shared his strategy for networking with me, and it was entirely focused on being a giver. He specifically waits one year before asking for ANY favor, big or small, from a new connection and instead focuses his efforts on things he can do for them. Can you add value and respect to a new relationship for a whole year without asking for anything? It won't be easy, and most of us likely won't be able to stick with it, but it's a great way to approach networking and begin your journey toward becoming a giver.

Another great strategy for adding value first is adding value on the spot. Simply ask the person if there is anything you can do for them, and then follow through on that action. It's important to refrain from talking about yourself and all of your accomplishments right away. When you follow through with instant value, it differentiates you from everybody else. Trust me, very few people do this.

Here are some ideas for how you can add value to a partnership or relationship

- Share contacts
- Offer expertise or knowledge
- Provide them with a new audience or bigger reach
- Write a testimonial or review
- Offer capital or an investment

- Barter services
- Reduce their suffering in a specific area (health, team-building, accounting)

Which of the two suggestions above would yield the biggest dividends for you within the next six months? Be sure to choose the ones that focus on your strengths.

_____

_____

_____

In addition to offering value, you must be unique in the way you let the individual know about your efforts. In my previous book, *6 Months to 6 Figures*, I provided the exact approach I used to connect with the unreachable of various industries, including Elon Musk, Arianna Huffington, Gary Vaynerchuk, Brian Tracy, Tim Ferriss, Eric Thomas, David Goggins, Isaiah Thomas, The Game (yes, the rapper), Mark Wahlberg, Kevin Gates, Jessica Alba, Ryan Garcia, and more. I was able to make connections with these influential individuals before I had achieved notoriety myself. It's a proven tactic that works regardless of career level or influence. Here, I've created a simplified version that's more reflective of modern-day email standards:

SUBJECT LINES
- Can I promote your work? (program, book, event, etc.)
- I want to help promote your brand!
- Paying you for your valuable time.
- Can I share your message?
- My audience would love to hear your message.

EMAIL BODY

Dear Achiever,

I respect your time at the highest level and won't ask for any of it! I know you get hundreds of messages weekly, so I wanted to take a different approach and let you know I've already [place the action you took here; see below for recommendations]

- Bought [number of] copies of your recent book
- Promoted [your product or service] to my audience of [the size and demographic of your audience]
- Shared your message on my social media
- Left you a review on Amazon and Audible
- Took the time to let [valuable connection] know about you

I want to thank you for all you do for others and ask if there is anything else I can do to add value, promote, or spread the word about your most recent work? I've been following you for quite some time now and love what you've created. Is there anything specific you're doing now that you're trying to promote, or something I can share?

I'm a big fan of your [insert relevant thing here: blog, book, product, event, etc.]. I particularly like your message about [insert their core message here], and it means a lot to me. I know it can be a thankless job being a role model/leader, so please know your work is making a massive difference in people's lives. It sure has in mine.

Anyway, since we're both in the business of [insert topic here], I thought I'd share your message with my audience, even if it's not as large as yours. Thanks again for all you do. Please let me know what you'd like for me to tell my audience and how I can help you. Looking forward to hearing from you!

Much Respect,
[your name here]

The above message works great as an email, but it can also be used to connect via social media as well. **Remember, one of the most important aspects of networking is making contact on multiple platforms.** Highly influential people get bombarded with so many requests each day they often miss or forget to respond to emails, so it's important for you to hit them from all angles. Check out their profiles on LinkedIn, Instagram, Facebook, and Twitter, and reach out on the one they use the most. Don't worry about annoying them with the multiple forms of outreach; successful people appreciate persistence and tenacity.

Another way to take action through your outreach is to offer to pay for the individual's time. While payment doesn't always guarantee a response, the simple act of *offering* to pay shows you're serious about your career, and you understand the value of their attention. It can also have a substantial payoff and result in you making more than you initially paid. For example, I paid my first mentor around $650 per month, and he ended up helping me make an extra $30k-40k that year. I then paid a multimillionaire $1,250 to $1,500 per month, and he took my income from six to seven figures. The expense may hurt a little at first but think of it as an investment in yourself. You've likely done this in other ways throughout your life, whether it was paying for an education, a personal trainer, or a class that taught you a new skill.

STEP 3. FOLLOW UP STRATEGICALLY AND CONSISTENTLY

A while back, one of our Academy-featured speakers, Ryan Serhant, star of *Million Dollar Listing New York*, said something that really struck me. *"Nobody likes to do business with just a networker."* In other words, the time you spend following up is equally important as making that initial contact.

This is just one of the many pieces of business genius insight Serhant has up his sleeve, all of which are featured in his *NYTimes* best-selling book, *Sell it Like Serhant*. On the subject of networking, he talks about the importance of the 3 F's strategy: Follow Up, Follow Through, and Follow Back.

1. Follow Up: This is the action you take after making your initial contact with a potential client or customer. You meet someone in an elevator or at an event, exchange information, and then BOOM! Send a follow-up email immediately and mention how great it was to meet them in person. Obviously, the content of your email will change with each encounter, but for the most part, it's along the lines of "Hey, great to meet you, would love to grab a coffee next week." It's brief, references your encounter, and then puts a future request or action into place. The goal with this "F" is to make a connection you can add to your referral network, which

is the network of people who will then refer you to their friends. This is applicable for ALL businesses, regardless of the industry. I've found time and time again that referrals and word-of-mouth marketing are always the most effective ways to generate new business.

2. **Follow Through:** This means staying true to your word and doing what you promised to do. If you made great contact through your follow-up and offered to assist them in some way (which I strongly recommend), then it's imperative that you follow through. Otherwise, you risk ruining your reputation and putting yourself farther back than if you had never made contact in the first place. Are you going to sell a house in X amount of time? Are you going to help someone lose five pounds within thirty days? Are you going to get somebody their first speaking gig? Are you going to make a beauty tutorial on YouTube featuring X? Whatever you promised, do it and then go the extra mile. This is a situation where you should underpromise and overdeliver.

3. **Follow Back:** This is the effort you put in to keep the conversation going. Even if the individual has decided against doing business with you, it's still essential to follow back as they may choose to do business with you in the future. Reach out to the clients you "lost," touch base with customers who were interested but never made a move, and engage with consumers who have previously come to you looking for advice, products, or services.

A great example of the importance of follow-up comes from my mom, Christina Voogd, a real estate agent who's been working on the Oregon coast for the past twenty years. She estimates that 95 percent of her customers are repeat customers due to her persistence in staying in contact. I recently asked her to disclose the details of the importance of follow-up. Here's what she said:

> "I work one sale at a time and give it 100 percent, no matter the price. Price has never mattered to me, and that's something I learned early on in my career. It's not about the immediate sale;

it's about building a long-term nest for the future. The relationship always comes before the transaction.

I've also found that by taking care of my small sales (and any sale, for that matter), I often get additional sales from my clients' friends and families, and eventually, I get repeat business. I'm to the point now where my business is run on referrals only. The past clients who purchase and sell again keep my business moving ahead.

I'm also the top agent in my town now, which comes from having a reputation for getting the job done, caring for my clients, and going the extra mile with exceptional service. For example, I recently sold a home to a client I worked with for over a year before the sale. Then, I sold a home to his brother. They decided to move their money out of California, and we've started closing on duplexes.

I also had two clients who looked at multiple homes over the course of a year but never ended up buying. I continued to stay in touch with them, and they eventually hired me to sell their home years later. This wouldn't have happened had I not stayed in touch or utilized a good follow-up system.

Staying in touch and consistently reaching out is what keeps me at the forefront of my client's minds. That leads to them recommending me to family and friends whenever the topic of real estate comes up."

Networking is a long-term game that requires continuous effort and attention, yet most of us give up before we've even started. We tend to interpret silence as rejection and act like teenagers with a crush. When we don't get a reply, we imagine a thousand reasons why we've been rejected, and most of them are reflections of our past.

I can tell you from personal experience that when someone fails to reply, it's rarely an active decision based on a dislike of your work. In fact, it generally doesn't have anything to do with you at all. There's a variety of reasons why someone might not respond, whether they're overloaded with their own work, your email got lost in their inbox, or your email may have gone to their spam folder. It's impossible to know, and therefore the lack of response should never be approached with emotion. Instead, use that energy to send follow-ups and continue to do so until you actually get a reply. It's not a sign of weakness, but rather of persistence and determination. If you don't let rejections deter your motivation, you'll find that most of them weren't really "rejections" at all.

One of the reasons my Business Manager Justin has become so valuable to our brand is because of the follow-up and follow-back systems he has created. For example, if we reach out to a potential guest speaker and they don't respond, the game never ends there. They continue to hear from us until we get a response, or until we've tried multiple platforms countless times, and we agree it's a dead end. The latter *rarely* occurs. Now keep in mind, being persistent is not as easy as just re-forwarding your email over and over again. Justin and I have developed countless follow-up scripts to reengage our targeted individuals, and we often personalize them with each send.

There is no one-size-fits-all follow-up/follow-back plan because creativity is the key, and you can never go wrong by making your messages relatable and relevant. You must show your contact you are committing the time and energy into communicating with them. Make it clear it's not just another spam email blast going out to thousands of people. Take the time to review the individual's social channels and any recent articles or media they have been featured in, and then utilize that information within your follow-up. For example, if the individual was just on vacation or finished up a big project, mention it in your email in a complimentary way. This proves to the reader you've done your homework and that you're worth a response.

One last important concept Justin incorporates into his follow-up communications is a clear articulation of "what's in it" for the reader. This isn't a situation where you should try to draw them in only to drop a big sales bomb later. You should never leave your reader guessing. Otherwise, they'll simply delete the email. If you're reaching out to someone about being on your podcast, don't just mention that you get 10,000 downloads per episode. Instead, give them the breakdown of your audience, the ways their episode will be distributed and promoted, and use your numbers to back it up. You'll also want to include details about what's required of them (how much of their time you'll need, the information you need, etc.) and the amount of work your team will be doing behind the scenes to ensure the episode gets maximum exposure. People want to know the facts up front; this reassures them that if they spend the time you're asking for, it won't be going to waste. Remember, they are likely thinking, "What's in it for me?"

ARE YOU READY TO CONQUER THE NETWORKING GAME?

Work on your list of ten dream mentors and contacts. Create a spreadsheet and list each of their communication channels. You'll be surprised how many "gurus" and millionaires respond to the contact form on their website. Look for social media channels, email addresses, and the real mailing address tied to their website. Going the extra mile can separate you from the herd.

I've created a networking blueprint called "The 3 Game-Changing Moves to Networking in the Digital Age," which has all the scripts I've used with my contacts. It also includes different approaches and a couple of other secrets I've used to get through to anybody. You can download it now at GameChangersMovement.com/Networking.

Use the execution plan on the following page to map out your strategy.

EXECUTION PLAN

Assess the current value of your network. Are you surrounding yourself with people who challenge you, make you think bigger, and elevate your standards?

_____

_____

_____

_____

Who are the friends, family, or associates that inspire you and challenge you to think bigger?

_____

_____

_____

_____

How can you strengthen your relationship with these people?

_____

_____

_____

_____

What is one change you can make to your social circle this week to bring you one step closer to your goals? If your schedule is already full of investing time in the wrong people, it's time to make room for people who can actually help you level-up your game.

_____

_____

_____

_____

What's currently missing from your networking strategy?

_____

_____

_____

_____

What's the next action you must take to become better at building your network?

_____

_____

_____

_____

CHAPTER 6

RULE 3

WORLD-CLASS FINANCIAL FREEDOM
AND WEALTH HABITS

> **Money without financial intelligence is money soon gone.**

IS AMERICA STILL THE LAND OF THE FREE? THE LAND OF OPPORTU-
nity? Can you build wealth that outlasts the tough times? The answer is
YES, but only if you adopt the right mindset and challenge certain ways
of thinking. According to *Forbes*, *Business Insider*, and *Yahoo Finance*, the
biggest transfer of wealth in US history has officially begun.

According to Fortune.com, there are 1,700 new millionaires created
every single day. That's 620,500 new millionaires per year, as in 620,500
individuals who have a net worth of over $1 million. Net worth is essen-
tially what you own minus what you owe. For example, if your only debt
comes from your mortgage, you'd subtract the amount you still owe on
your mortgage from the amount of your total cash flow, including sav-
ings, retirement, etc.

While the above statistics may seem startling, being a millionaire is still pretty rare in our country: only 3 percent of our population has a seven-figure net worth. This means that 97 percent of us will spend a good portion of our lives striving to reach this status but will fail to come out on top. I don't say this as a means of discouragement, but rather as a realistic, eye-opening piece of insight. We're all capable of being part of that 3 percent, but it requires patience, determination, and an unrelenting focus on the end goal.

I do want to make one thing clear before we delve further into this chapter: this book isn't just about making more money. It's about interrupting the belief system you currently have and propelling you toward real, sustainable wealth. You won't get to seven figures with the same tactics you used to achieve six figures, nor will you find these strategies in an overcomplicated financial book. Instead, we'll take some of the mental strategies we've covered in previous chapters and combine them with a few financial tips and tricks I've learned over the past fifteen years. By the end of this chapter, you should have a clear understanding of how to build both personal and financial wealth at a truly World-Class level.

THE WEALTH COMPLEX

I've had love and respect for money since the age of fifteen when I first set my sights on a pair of Air Jordan's and made my first profit online. The profit from selling shoes on eBay allowed me to escape the hard labor I couldn't stand doing. I had such an infatuation with those shoes, it was almost as if they provided me with a purpose in life. It seems silly looking back on it now, but as a child, I didn't fully understand the value of money and simply wanted what every kid wants: adoration from my peers. This mentality followed me into my twenties but was executed at a much greater expense. I purchased fancy cars, designer clothing, and lavish vacations. You name it, I bought it. It was as if I had an unrelenting need to leave a lasting impression on everyone I met, and I genuinely believed material objects could help me achieve that. I can't say for certain if this method rang true, but I do know having a wealth-obsessed mentality played a major role in helping me to develop a strong work ethic. I realized later it wasn't just the money I was after; it was the choices, flexibility, and freedom it brought to my life.

Now that I'm older and have a wife, son, and another on the way, my priorities have shifted significantly, but I still have a deep, underlying respect and appreciation for money. My priorities have shifted more toward lifestyle, leverage, freedom, and autonomy, and these are the main reasons I became an entrepreneur. I wanted the freedom to do what I wanted, when I wanted, and where I wanted on my terms. Not just for me, but for my family as well. Through previous experience and self-awareness, I knew I was unemployable. I knew I didn't like others telling me what to do, and I didn't enjoy the "hard labor" route. Learning how to make and respect money saved my life, and it's allowed my family to have massive freedom, flexibility, and peace of mind.

This isn't something I feel the need to apologize for, but I understand why these might be perceived as negative qualities. There's a strong stigma surrounding the concept of wealth in our country, much of which is completely justified. We've seen how much power it can provide and how quickly that power can be abused, whether through corrupt wall street schemes, political campaigns, or celebrity bribes. And while it might be easy to point blame at a person's net worth, I can confidently tell you that wealth is not the cause of these issues in our country. Rather, it's the values and personal decisions of certain individuals—those who fail to lead a World-Class and purpose-driven life.

So, with that, I want you to ask yourself the following:

Why not become wealthy?

Why not become a millionaire?

Why not become financially free, so my entire family has more choices?

Why not be able to do what I want, when I want, wherever I want, on my terms?

I've been on both sides of the financial spectrum. I know what it's like to be dead broke with no choices, to feel constantly stressed about my next bill, and I've experienced the utter shame of not being able to afford an appetizer at a restaurant. I also know what it's like to acquire massive wealth and then quickly lose it all—that's just the pendulum of entrepreneurship. However, now that I'm on the other side and I'm able to live my life without the threat of going broke, I can say with certainty that I prefer this lifestyle MUCH more than the former. Do I still have some of the problems I had when I was broke? Of course! Money doesn't solve everything. But thanks to my financial stability, I'm now able to focus on the things that bring me a true sense of fulfillment in life, making those problems far more bearable.

I share these personal experiences to emphasize the importance of appreciating wealth. This isn't to say it should rule your life, but you must be capable of visualizing yourself as a wealthy individual without losing your moral compass or letting the perception of others get in the way. The road to fortune comes with a lot of dips, curves, and disappointments, and a majority of people will give up before they reach the finish line. However, by appreciating the effort required to attain wealth, you'll be much less likely to fail. Money is an excellent servant but a terrible master.

> **Money can't buy you happiness, but with the right perspective, it can buy you massive freedom.**

UNDERSTANDING FINANCIAL STRUGGLE

"Some of my friends are poor; all they have is money."
—Paulo Coelho

To create your roadmap for acquiring wealth, it's important to first address some of the primary causes associated with financial struggle. This might seem like a contradictory place to start, but it's important to understand any potential problem areas within your own financial approach before delving into a strategy. This also offers a unique opportunity to jump ahead of the struggle while the rest of society focuses on staying afloat. During the toughest of times, money doesn't disappear—it just transfers to those who know how to avoid pitfalls.

The causes listed below come from my own personal observations, as well as hundreds of conversations I've had with some of today's most financially successful entrepreneurs. See if any of them apply to you.

CAUSE 1: ASSUMING AGE DETERMINES VALUE

We see proof of this every day on multiple platforms. The traditional path of becoming wealthy—i.e., working your way up and then making it big at age fifty—is now a thing of the past, thanks to the mass capabilities of the internet. I personally know seventeen- and eighteen-year-olds making hundreds of thousands of dollars annually, millionaires who are just reaching age twenty, and quite a few baby boomers who are broke. It might be hard to accept, but it's simply the new way of our economy. The wealthy are both wealthier and younger, and the poor are poorer and older.

A survey of US investors with $25 million or more found the average age of investors has decreased by eleven years since 2014 to age forty-seven, and it will likely continue to drop in the years to come. These wealthy Americans, whose ranks have more than doubled since the depths of the Great Recession, are typically younger than less wealthy millionaires. The finding suggests a "vast generational transfer of wealth is just beginning," says George Walper Jr., President of the Spectrem Group, the company which conducted the study.

I recently bought a condo and some land in Tulum, Mexico, as it's become one of my wife's and my favorite destinations to visit. I've built a great network of developers and business professionals in the Riviera Maya and recently found out the most common investors in that area are millennials: digital nomads, entrepreneurs, artists, and creatives between the ages of twenty-six and thirty-four.

CAUSE 2: PRIORITIZING CERTIFICATIONS OVER SKILLS

Yes, the number of millionaires may be rising, but not necessarily due to their traditional education. In fact, many of today's largest and most successful companies, including Google, IBM, Apple, and more, no longer require degrees for employment and accept applicants with equivalent practical experience. Consider when you graduated from college. Did you feel completely prepared to jump into a high-paying job head-first? Probably not. You likely learned many of the skills you use today through experience or trial and error.

In the modern-day workforce, companies can no longer rely on fil-tering applications based on college education, as many colleges also use outdated, irrelevant curriculums.

The fact that we're not educated on the concept of money in school is an injustice to our country, and why we see such a significant income gap. Rather than being taught the Pythagorean theorem or how to dis-sect a frog, why weren't we taught the following:

- Taxes and the importance of building credit
- How to build wealth and invest
- How to become more valuable or even irreplaceable
- How to lead and solve problems
- The importance of networking and building relationships
- How to debate
- The importance of emotional maturity

The only means we have for learning about money is the financial experience and knowledge of our parents, and as a result, most of us are stuck in an endless loop of multigenerational debt. I was fortunate to have parents who taught me the value of investing, as well as the value of having good credit at a young age, but I know many individuals who weren't so lucky and now face many of the same problems their parents did.

This isn't to say that having a college degree offers no value; it just depends on your profession. However, does it provide the same value as the initial investment required to attain it? Probably not. It also provides a false notion of job security, which is a concept that is nearly nonexis-tent in our technologically-fueled society. Why didn't anybody tell me that by the time I was an adult, a large percentage of jobs would either be performed by robots or sent overseas? Or that much of the history I spent so many years learning about could eventually be searched for with the push of a button on a keyboard? Or that we would eventually have one of the most unstable job markets in nearly a century, with new industries and technological advances shifting our economy nearly every six months?

And here's why I'm frustrated. Despite these factors, we're still pushing our children through the same routine curriculum our grandparents had and then watching them face the inevitable consequences: a lack of real-world skills, a mountain of debt, and not enough financial know-how to pay it off.

CAUSE 3: NOT RESPECTING OR VALUING MONEY

We've all fantasized about waking up and seeing our bank account filled with more zeros than we could ever imagine. There are entire books dedicated to exactly that: becoming a massive overnight success. In reality, however, earning a mass amount of money before having a true appreciation for it could hurt your future more than not having it at all.

A good example of this is what happens among lottery winners. In a recent study conducted by the American Economic Association, findings show that an average of 70 percent of lottery winners end up going broke within a matter of three to five years and that most only save a mere sixteen cents for every dollar won. Other studies have found that instead of getting people out of financial trouble, winning the lottery gets people into more trouble because bankruptcy rates soared for lottery winners within three to five years after winning. [3]

Another example of this rapid depletion of money occurs among pro athletes. According to *Sports Illustrated*, **78 percent** of NFL players are either bankrupt or are under financial stress within two years after retirement. An estimated **60 percent** of NBA players are broke within five years after retirement, even though the average NBA player makes almost $30 million over the life of their career, not counting

---

3   Loewenstein, George. "Perspective | Five Myths about the Lottery." *The Washington Post*, WP Company, 27 Dec. 2019, www.washingtonpost.com/outlook/five-myths/five-myths-about-the -lottery/2019/12/27/742b9662-2664-11ea-ad73-2fd294520e97_story.html.

endorsements and brand deals. Needless to say, making money at a young age or being paid for talent rather than a learned skill can be a dangerous game and often leads to blind, impulsive spending without considering the consequences.

Take former LA Clipper Darius Miles, for instance. He was drafted straight out of high school in 2000 and was paid $3 million for his first year, not including endorsements, shoe deals, commercials, etc. By his final season in 2009, he was taking home $10 million annually. Overall, he earned $68 million throughout the course of his career. Fast-forward eleven years to 2020, and his net worth is negative one million.

How does something like this even happen? How can someone have SO much and later end up with so little?

In a 2018 interview, Darius stated:

> "When you're young, you think the money is gonna last forever. I don't care how street smart you are or who you got in your corner. When you go from not having anything to making millions of dollars at 18, 19 years old, you're not going to be prepared for it. If you read the headlines about me now, it's all about me going bankrupt. People ask me, 'Man, how can you lose all that money?' That part is easy to explain. You already heard that story a million times, with a million players. The cliché is that guys go broke buying Ferraris or whatever. Listen, it takes a long time to go broke buying Ferraris. What makes you go broke are shady business deals. They'll make the money disappear quickly."

The important message to take away from the above scenarios is that money without financial intelligence is money soon gone. It may seem fun to be given a large sum of money without putting in much effort, but that time and effort are what help us develop a careful appreciation for money and a better understanding of how to use it.

Now that you understand these three causes of financial struggle, it should be clear as to why most of society is in debt and confused about how to become financially free, as well as the areas where you can move and rise above. Ultimately, you have to understand how money works before you make it. You have to understand why most are struggling before you can thrive. And you have to understand how to play the game before you can change it.

CREATING WORLD-CLASS WEALTH

We often only hear about how much the economy is suffering. Whether it's lack of jobs, a dwindling stock market, or our country's mounting debt, making a large sum of money in this day and age might seem like a hopeless effort. However, consider these numbers:

- **$1.5 trillion:** The amount of US money currently in circulation as of September 2020—most of it in the form of Federal Reserve notes. If you're wondering what Federal Reserve notes are and where you might see them, check your wallet. It's the fancy term for US currency.
- **$70 trillion:** All of the world's stock markets contain about $70 trillion worth of company shares, and roughly half of them are for US-based companies. That's not so surprising, considering we have some enormous companies.
- **$81 trillion:** The estimated amount of money in circulation throughout the entire world, but only counting coins, bills, and bank deposits. This does not include other assets of value.
- **$1.2 quadrillion:** The amount of money estimated to be invested in derivatives or financial products which can be quite complicated. It's an immensely large number, alternatively written as $1,200,000,000,000,000. And here's a mind-blowing fact: more money is invested in derivatives than in all of the world's stock markets combined.

This information tells us there is no shortage of money in the American economy; there's only a shortage of people willing to change and conceptualize how to become more valuable as entrepreneurs. If you happen to be dissatisfied with your income, you might investigate all of your excuses. Lack of awareness causes financial turmoil, and people in poverty usually have a wealth of excuses and often validate them by telling themselves that money is evil. However, by shifting your perspective and following the tips below, you can forge a path toward sustainable, World-Class wealth.

I. QUESTION EVERYTHING

If we learned anything from the financial crash of 2008, it's that previously "secure" financial traditions aren't necessarily applicable in the modern-day economy. We've been led to believe that owning a home means long-term stability, putting our money in banks means guaranteed security, and having a 401k leads to a stress-free retirement, but that's no longer the way of the world. The best thing you can do for your financial future is to continuously conduct your due diligence and question everything. Our financial and economic systems set our society up to fail, and the only way to come out on top is to recognize the illusions and understand that no one understands your financial situation better than you.

As Ronald Reagan said, "Trust, but verify."

2. SAVE TO INVEST, AND BE PURPOSEFUL

We are taught from an early age to save, save, and save. I didn't even hear about the importance of investing until I was twenty. Saving doesn't make you more money, it doesn't compound, and it only maintains your lifestyle at best. Saving without investing is an old adage that needs to be updated to what is relevant and working NOW. You'll become far wealthier if you learn to invest, regardless of what you do to earn money along the way.

In one of my recent interviews with Robert Kiyosaki, author of *Rich Dad Poor Dad*, one of the books that changed my life at age eighteen, he stated:

> "My poor dad always said, 'Work hard and save money.' Yet, he didn't follow his own advice. His lack of financial intelligence led him to make poor money choices, draining his savings. He was one type of smart person who does not save.
>
> My rich dad always said, 'If you want to be wealthy and finan-

cially secure, working hard and saving money will not get you there.' He did follow his own advice. Rather than save money, he invested it. As a result, he grew his money exponentially and became financially independent at a young age. He was also a type of smart person who does not save. When it came to being smart, I modeled my smarts after my rich dad. Today, I am also financially independent. But I know many other smart people who also do not save—but only because they squander their money on liabilities rather than investing it in assets.

At the end of the day, why do people save? For most, it's in preparation for retirement, but most of us know that saving is not enough to prepare for a secure retirement. This is especially true for young people who will never see a pension from their employer.

Today, everyone is expected to invest in a secure retirement. Unfortunately, our schools do not prepare us to invest wisely, or even at all. So, it's up to us to become financially educated and teach our children financial education as well. This is something the wealthy have done for generations."

3. LIVE BELOW YOUR MEANS

If you can't buy it twice in cash, you can't afford it.

This is one of the most important wealth habits I didn't fully understand until much later in my career, and it's been a huge game-changer. As I stated earlier, I've had a love for high- price items since I was young and have done my fair share of splurging. However, the more I surrounded myself with wealthy individuals, the more I started to realize they didn't possess this same infatuation with luxury items—most were living well below their means. It was then that I learned a simple mantra that completely changed my thought process about financial management:

> **"Think like the millionaires, but hustle like you're broke until the wealth catches up."**

That's exactly what I did in 2013 when I moved from Washington to California. I was making the most money I had ever made in my career, yet rather than purchasing a fancy BMW, I purchased an old Honda Civic and invested the rest of my money back into my business and into real estate. I didn't know it at the time, but this was one of the biggest game-changing moves of my career.

This is a common practice among many successful individuals. So much, in fact, they're often referred to as "undercover millionaires" due to how little they show off their wealth. An extreme example of this is Warren Buffet, the third-richest man in the world. He has a net worth of $86 billion yet still lives in Omaha, Nebraska, in a home he purchased in 1958 for just $31,500. Another example is former Microsoft CEO Steve Ballmer. He's also worth billions yet has been known to fly commercial. These individuals understand that while they could easily afford mansions and private jets, it's far more lucrative to invest that money back into their businesses or assets that work for them.

What this method also proves is that being a millionaire is more about who you become rather than what you have. The real fun in success doesn't come from spending your cash the moment you make it—it comes from figuring out how to make more and multiply it, which requires self-discipline and a constant focus on the future. When you start to change your priorities, you'll start to change your life. Your desire to build wealth has to exceed your desire to buy expensive things too soon.

4. MAKE YOUR MONEY WORK FOR YOU

One of the biggest differences between the wealthy and those who struggle is that wealthy people earn interest while everyone else *pays* interest. To reach financial independence, your money has to work for you—not you for it.

"Make your money work for you" is such common money advice that it borders on being cliché. But what does it actually mean? And more importantly, how can you do it? There's no simple answer nor single way to do it, but to reach true financial independence, you need to take action on this concept. There are a lot of ways you can make your money work for you. With the right systems, you can save and invest for your future. Doing so will build a solid foundation for your personal finances. I will walk through a couple of my favorite ways later in this chapter.

5. CREATE MULTIPLE STREAMS OF INCOME

As you begin to invest, it's important to diversify your portfolio. You never want to invest all of your money in just one avenue, and especially not in just one business. Also, you may get to the point where you want to purchase investments that generate income for you. Many people consider real estate a good option for such an investment because it generates a reliable, monthly income. I talk about having multiple streams of income a lot because I believe it's the most efficient way to build wealth, and I'm not the only one. Researchers have even pinpointed a statistic: millionaires, on average, have not just one, but *seven* different streams of income.

So, how many do you have?

Whether it's one or fifteen, the number doesn't matter right now. What matters is your next move. I remember having zero sources of income and feeling down and out, but once I created one that was sustained and systemized, I was then able to focus on my next one, and I built it gradually from there. It's important to remember that every individual who has multiple streams of income once started with zero.

Below is a list of four things World-Class entrepreneurs invest their money into, which will give you more clarity around your own investing.

THE FOUR THINGS WORLD-CLASS ENTREPRENEURS SPEND MONEY ON

"Reinvesting your profits is the best way to build wealth."
—Warren Buffett

A major component in developing strategic financial habits is knowing where to invest your money, both in business and in life. There are a lot of choices out there, and one wrong move can mean the difference between going broke and making it big, so how do you choose?

While the answer might be different for each of us, there are four primary things that successful entrepreneurs always spend money on due to the undeniable benefits they offer.

I. PERSONAL DEVELOPMENT

Successful entrepreneurs invest in training, mentorship, seminars, books, and anything that sharpens their perspective and cuts their learning curve in half. These are things that can save you time, money, and energy and help you foresee pitfalls that others have fallen into. In business, speed is important, and you pay for speed by educating yourself and being able to anticipate what's coming.

I sought out my first mentor in 2008, and while it was a costly investment at the time, it proved to be well worth it. Having a mentor gave me access to a broader network and helped me avoid many potentially costly and time-consuming mistakes. Even now, at the most successful point in my career, I still have a mentor. Not because I need business advice, necessarily, but because I work more efficiently when I have someone to help me bounce ideas around. That's what investing in yourself is about—recognizing the things that help you operate at peak performance or speed up your learning curve and making them a consistent part of your financial budget.

As the great Jim Rohn once said, "Work harder on yourself than you do on your job. If you work hard on your job, you'll make a living, but if you work hard on yourself, you'll make a fortune."

So, what personal investments should you make? It depends on what you need and what your specific goals are. You're looking for the things that will speed up your learning curve and help you achieve your goals quicker. This isn't about cutting corners; it's about being intelligent with your time, energy, and resources.

Things to think about:

- Make sure everything you invest in is proven, relevant, and congruent to your life, business vision, and values.
- Make sure the person teaching practices what they preach, is a World-Class human being, and has the results you are striving for.

- Ask yourself if you've taken action on the previous information you've learned before moving on to new content.
- Do your due diligence and make sure it's the best training available for the specific topic or area you want to improve on.

2. BUSINESS GROWTH

For any business that's looking to grow, some form of reinvestment is necessary. While this doesn't mean you have to reinvest all of your profits, investing a significant amount of resources can dramatically improve your bottom line and position your business for long-term growth. In general, most startups and newer businesses invest about 90 percent of their profits back into their business, whether through marketing, websites, supplies, etc. However, it may be different for your business. The key is having a full-scope understanding of your finances as well as your future plans, so your reinvestment is as lucrative and beneficial as possible. Don't ever put yourself in a position where there aren't enough funds to cover other expenses, especially the ones that have proven results and produce profits.

So, what type of business expenses are considered to be smart investments? Marketing, for starters. An effective marketing campaign is crucial for business growth and will almost always pay off if executed correctly. The biggest mistake most new businesses make is throwing a random sum of money toward marketing but then failing to track the results. That's essentially money down the drain. If marketing isn't something you're skilled in or have the time or resources to learn about, then invest those funds into paying a marketing agency or expert. It's important to quantify the results you can expect, so you will be able to monitor the success of the campaign. Consider how many leads it might bring, and in turn, how those leads will increase your sales. Data is key.

There are only three ways to grow your business. You can increase the number of clients, increase the average sale price, or increase the number of times your clients buy in a year. Most people (90 percent) focus on increasing the number of clients, and this method is the least effective and the least profitable. So, I recommend spending some time effectively increasing the other two.

It's also important to invest in staff and build a strong team that's aligned with your vision and values. This may vary based on your industry, business model, and overall vision, but big growth often requires great people. Large-scale companies with excess funds often use the "hire fast and fire slow" model because it's more time-efficient in the short-term. However, if you're just starting out, I encourage you to do the opposite. Take your time in finding the right people for your team and cut dead weight as quickly as possible.

On that note, it's also important to invest in your time. Remember: time isn't money. Money is money, and time is time, but time invested strategically makes a lot more money. Spending a small percentage of your profits to free yourself up can be a significant investment. By outsourcing your administrative tasks, customer service, bookkeeping, marketing, etc., you can focus on the things that are more directly related to growth, such as sales or strategy development. Your ultimate goal should be to work *on* the business, not *in* it.

3. ASSETS (MAKING YOUR MONEY WORK FOR YOU)

Being financially successful means being actively involved with your money and understanding what your assets are doing. It's about having a budget, tracking spending, consistently contributing to investments, and always planning ahead to avoid financial downfalls. However, the key to establishing World-Class wealth is to make smart, strategic investments that continuously compound and increase even while you sleep. If you're simply trading time for money, you'll never be able to get ahead. You must learn how to leverage your money in a way that works for you personally.

Some examples are:

- Angel investing
- Real estate
  - › Short-term and long-term rentals
  - › Multifamily
  - › Residential or commercial
  - › Duplexes

> › Fix-and-flips
> › Vacation rentals (Airbnb)
- Art
- Classic cars
- Membership sites

As long as the investment appreciates over time, it's likely a safe bet. One of my personal favorites is real estate. I've purchased five properties within the last year alone, and they've not only been a great source of additional income, but they've also diversified my financial portfolio. My wife and I have close to twenty properties in multiple states and one property out of the country. We have a goal of making $1 million per year in residual income.

4. MEMORABLE AND INSPIRING EXPERIENCES

When is the last time you had a truly memorable experience? Would you take a vacation if you knew it would directly increase your profits? Well lucky for you, it can, and smart millionaires know all about this.

In a new CNBC millionaire Survey, it showed that people with seven-figure incomes had the highest number of home improvement and vacation purchases. Half of these millionaires spent at least $2,500 on home improvements, and about 60 percent spent at least $5,000 on vacations. The fact that more than half spent double on vacations than on their own home makes one thing very clear: you can't put a price tag on an experience.

Taking the time to explore the world, experience different cultures, and meet new people opens you up in ways that nothing else can. It gives you a deeper perspective of the human condition, which can translate to better targeting strategies for your business. In addition, traveling is a great way to recover from burnout and do a system reset for your body and brain, which in turn will help you make smarter business decisions. There's also the motivation factor. Personally, I don't think there's anything more motivating than being able to take loved ones on an unforgettable vacation. It reminds you of all your hard work and will keep you focused on getting results in your life and business. Just imagine being able to take your family on an all-expenses-paid, ten-day cruise or a trip to Hawaii without having to worry about finances. To some of you, that might seem like an unrealistic fantasy, but why not turn it into your reality?

Whether you're rich, poor, or have experienced both, the most important takeaway I hope you get from this chapter is that being rich isn't all about money. It's about peace of mind, abundance, time freedom, success, and living well. There are plenty of rich people living a poor life due to having the wrong mindset or incongruent values. By learning how to change your perspective, you can carve your own path toward establishing true, World-Class wealth. The difference between ordinary and extraordinary income is fast implementation. How quickly will you get on your grind to start increasing your income? Your bank account isn't who you are; it reflects who you were before you made the decision to focus on building real wealth.

Let's start building your wealth right away. Use the execution plan on the following page to craft your perfect action.

EXECUTION PLAN

Have you ever thought about what real wealth means to you? Define what real financial freedom and wealth mean to you.

_____

_____

_____

_____

_____

It's impossible to track the future if you don't know where you started. Your first step is to track how much money you've invested in yourself, your business, assets, and World-Class experiences. If you don't have perfect financial records, do your best to estimate how much you've spent in each of these four key areas in the past twelve months.

Personal Development _____

Business _____

Assets _____

World-Class Experiences _____

What were your ten largest purchases in the last twelve months? Did you buy "things" that made you feel good at the time, and now you barely remember them? Or did you buy assets that will appreciate and compound over time?

1. _____

2. _____

3. _____

4. _____

5. _____

6. _____

7. _____

8. _____

9. _____

10. _____

Connecting your investing, wealth-building, and your dreams is a big part of becoming wealthy. What are your top five financial goals for the next twelve months? How much do you want to earn? How much do you want to invest? How much do you want to make per month? How much liquid cash?

_____

_____

_____

_____

_____

_____

Going forward, keep track of your finances using accounting software or a spreadsheet. Make each financial decision with intent. Plan in advance how much you will invest in each category, and then stick to your plan. A year from now, you want to be able to look back and see that you invested your money wisely. I've found that those who've made the most money and created the most wealth are the ones who know their numbers inside and out. Business owners who don't know the math of their business are not managing their business; they are guessing their business.

RULE 4

WORLD-CLASS HUSTLE AND GRIND
(THE RIGHT VEHICLE)

"None are more hopelessly enslaved than those who falsely believe they are free."
—JOHANN WOLFGANG VON GOETHE

EXPRESSING YOUR DESIRE TO BE AN ENTREPRENEUR A MERE TEN TO fifteen years ago would have been met with laughter and the assumption that you're crazy. The tables have turned, and entrepreneurship has now become one of the most respected and intelligent paths to take. It has saved our economy, and it continues to push our culture forward. "Dream jobs" are disappearing fast, while creating your "ideal opportunity" seems to be the new normal. I truly believe there is only one real success: living life your own way, on your terms.

Most people believe they are free, yet others still tell them when to work, when they can leave, what they can do, how they should do it, and how much they're worth. If it's your future, why would you put somebody else in control? Enough is enough. Stop being a slave to your job and create your own opportunities where you live each and every day doing exactly what you want to do. If you love your reality, you'll never want to escape it. It's very common in our society for most people to validate fear by playing small. There are also a lot of people justifying getting their rights taken away. Real freedom is having complete autonomy in how you live, as well as the choices you make.

What's more important: the journey or the destination?

The answer is neither if you don't have the right vehicle.

In this case, the term "vehicle" refers to a job, career, or opportunity, and having the right one means having a vehicle that's congruent with your values and vision; something that will keep you fascinated and engaged for the next five to ten years.

But Peter, how can I think five to ten years down the line when I don't know what's going on next month?

Well, what's the alternative?

Just like activities that aren't connected to an outcome, having a vehicle that isn't connected to a purpose is the drain of all fulfillment, peace of mind, happiness, and motivation. When you aren't happy or fulfilled, you aren't resourceful or creative, which leads to an endless loop of frustration both in business and in life. When it comes to your future, direction is more important than speed.

Remember, how you do anything is how you do everything. Most people have built their lifestyle around their business and put their work first due to necessity. However, it's now more possible than ever to build a career that integrates with your lifestyle and priorities, which is a far more fulfilling way to live. This isn't to say you can't put your work first or you shouldn't be obsessed with your career. This simply means we now have the resources and flexibility to design both the lifestyle and business we truly desire.

This is a fairly new concept that some people may not fully agree with due to their generational beliefs or upbringing. Just a mere twenty to twenty-five years ago, the common theme was to do what society expected of you, no questions asked. You were taught to be happy with what you had, respect your boss, work your way up the ladder, and follow the rules. And if you didn't like your job or had a boss that made your life hell, it didn't matter. You had to tolerate it the same way everyone else did because it was the norm.

I'm here to tell you those times are over, and younger generations have already carved a path for change. According to odesk.com, 89 percent of millennials prefer to choose when and where they work, rather than being placed in a 9-to-5 position, and 45 percent of them choose workplace flexibility over increased pay. In other words, younger generations are now choosing autonomy over security and happiness over success. As a result, they're now making leaps and bounds in new, inventive industries, while older generations struggle to keep up.

It's time to stop thinking and living like it's 1995 and realize how unique this moment in time really is. More importantly, it's time to break out of the traditional box that's held our dreams and ambitions captive for so long. I see so many people held back by the fear of failure, or even the fear of success—almost as if they're comforted by their own insecurities. In reality, however, those insecurities prolong living a life that was built by someone else.

With that, I challenge you to have faith in your abilities and chase the unknown. I can say with 100 percent certainty that ANYTHING is possible when you start to value your dreams and goals over your excuses and fear. You just have to be willing to look and learn how to use your resources.

Let's walk through some of the benefits of having the right vehicle.

BENEFITS OF HAVING THE RIGHT VEHICLE

Fulfillment: Waking up excited and eager for the day ahead is a priceless feeling and one of the biggest benefits of having the right vehicle. You'll also find yourself more naturally engaged and present in your work, as you'll be feeding your internal need for fulfillment.

Values: In Chapter 4, we talked about defining your values and living in alignment with what's most important to you. That's what finding the right vehicle is all about. You want to make sure the career you choose, the opportunities you take on, or the business you start matches your values and lifestyle. Otherwise, you could find yourself right back where you started: miserable, stressed, and constrained.

Long-Term Engagement and Fascination: We've all fallen victim to the "grass is always greener" mentality or "shiny object" syndrome. It's human nature. Although when you work in an industry that you find both fascinating and challenging, the constant need to jump to the next new thing will no longer be an issue. Distraction comes when our brain doesn't get the activity it craves, so as long as you do work that you love, patience and focus will come naturally. The grass isn't greener on the other side; the grass is greener where you water it. If you've completely sold yourself on your vehicle and continuously work on yourself, the "grass is greener" mentality isn't as common.

Control: When you choose the right vehicle, you're always in control; you're no longer at the mercy of a higher-up. The best entrepreneurs control their business, their income, and their financial future. In *The Millionaire Fastlane*, MJ DeMarco says, "When you bequeath control to others, you essentially become a hitchhiker with no seat belt. You take the passenger seat in a stranger's car, which could be murderous to your financial plan. And when that happens, you're vulnerable to joining the ranks of victims." You want to do everything possible to be 100 percent in control of your future, your finances, and your schedule. If you're at the mercy of a social media platform, an affiliate partner, or a boss, one quick change could mean you're out of business. I've seen this happen all too often.

These are just a few of the benefits of choosing the right vehicle. Writer Annie Dillard famously said, "How we spend our days is, of course, how we spend our lives." For many of us, a large portion of our days is spent at work. In fact, the average person will spend 90,000 hours at work over a lifetime. It's safe to say that the vehicle you choose will have a huge impact on the quality of your life.

EVERYTHING BEGINS WITH YOUR STANDARDS

Are your standards high enough?

I'm not referring to your standards for your lifestyle, family, or friends. I'm talking about your standards for *yourself.*

This is one of the most important aspects in creating a roadmap for change, yet one that we ignore the most. The standards we set for ourselves or what we're willing to tolerate often determine how our life turns out. When you become complacent, you stay complacent. It's that simple. In order to create change, you must understand the standards you need to elevate within and force yourself to stop tolerating mediocre results.

Here are some examples:

- If you tolerate making only $50k a year, you have little chance of making $100k.
- If you tolerate making a comfortable six-figure income, you'll never make it to seven.
- If you allow yourself to fall into the complacency of society, you'll never know what you're truly capable of.
- If you tolerate being disrespected, you'll always be disrespected.
- If you tolerate being overworked and underpaid, you'll always be overworked and underpaid.
- If you tolerate being overweight and unhealthy, you'll always be overweight and unhealthy.
- If you tolerate mediocrity and average results, you'll always be mediocre and get average results.
- If you tolerate being broke and stressed, you'll always be broke and stressed.

You will always get what you tolerate and think you're worthy of. The value comes in when you rewire your thinking and stop tolerating the things you know you shouldn't, whether it's a disrespectful boss, an abusive spouse, an unhealthy lifestyle, poor results, or a failing business. It's not about public perception or what others expect of you; it's about what you expect from yourself. If your business has been hovering around the $750,000 mark for the past couple of years due to your complacency, it's time to step it up, even if you're doing better than the majority. Remember, the only person you should compare yourself to is the person you were yesterday.

> **"Enough is enough" can be a life-altering statement.**

Let's dive deeper by figuring out the areas where you've been complacent.

"It's my standards that make me successful. Every day I demand more from myself than anybody else could humanly expect from me. I'm not competing against anybody else; I'm competing with what I am capable of."

—**Michael Jordan**

What are you currently tolerating that you shouldn't? What isn't serving you well?

_____

_____

_____

How much will your life and happiness be affected if you keep tolerating those things over the next couple of years?

_____

_____

_____

What areas of your life should you raise your standards in?

_____

_____

_____

Gaining awareness of your current standards can be extremely beneficial. When you expand your awareness and conceptualize what you've been tolerating, it's easier to recognize what you _shouldn't_ be tolerating, which sets you ahead of the curve tenfold. Most of our society is content with mediocrity, and why wouldn't they be? It's a comfortable place to be that doesn't require change or effort. But then, as a society, we see stats like this:

- According to Forbes.com, 76 percent of people hate what they do and are actively disengaged at work.

- A quarter of Americans say work is their number one source of stress.
- Last year, Americans used an average of seventeen vacation days, which is less than the average of twenty days used in the 1980s and 1990s.
- Sixty percent of college grads can't find work after they've gone into $40-100k of debt
- Only 2 percent of our society is financially stable at age sixty-five.
- One in three Americans believes their best chance of becoming wealthy is to win the lottery.
- In 2020 the average price of college had increased 27 percent, while the average student income is at an all-time low.

These stats wouldn't exist if we didn't work so hard to avoid progress, although it's really no fault of our own. Our schools have been teaching kids how to fit in and conform, not to stand out and lead. In addition, most of our parents come from a generation of conformists, the ones who created the dry, in-the-box school curriculum. And unless there's one black sheep in the family to break the mold, all future generations are likely to follow suit.

Making the transition from a traditional 9-to-5 employee to a self-employed entrepreneur isn't easy by any means. It can be stressful, isolating, and feel like a never-ending uphill battle. But once you push past the frustrations and start challenging your old way of thinking, you can create a new, exciting path full of unlimited opportunities—one that allows for growth, fulfillment, and tremendous upside.

CREATING YOUR UNSTOPPABLE ROADMAP

"A genius without a roadmap will get lost in any country, but an average person with a roadmap will find their way to any destination."
—Brian Tracy

It took a total mind-transformation for me to realize what I was capable of and what I wanted out of life. I had a lot of moments of self-doubt and anxiety about my decision to pursue entrepreneurship full-time. But once I finally found my vehicle, everything else became easier to figure out.

In this section, we'll define your ideal outcome and then craft an unstoppable roadmap for your future. We'll use a reverse-engineering method in which we start with your end goal and *then* define the smaller goals required to get there. This not only helps you gain clarity but also keeps the bigger picture—or finale—at the forefront.

Keep in mind there is no set time frame for this, nor is there a proven method that works for everyone. The important thing is to continue pushing yourself forward and to use any and all available resources until you've reached a point of complete clarity.

In Chapter 4, we walked you through a series of questions to help you gain clarity. If you haven't worked through these yet, I want you to read Chapter 4 again and make sure you've completed all the exercises. You either have self-awareness and clarity, or you don't.

Answering the questions below will help you make concrete, definitive decisions for your life and business, which is a common characteristic of successful individuals. They make decisions quickly using the information they have, and once their decision is made, it's difficult to change it. On the contrary, average people tend to make decisions slowly and change their minds rapidly, resulting in a web of unclear thoughts and self-doubt.

So, with that, let's start charting your roadmap.

AN HONEST ASSESSMENT OF YOUR CURRENT REALITY

On a scale of 1-10, how important is money to you? _____
On a scale of 1-10, how important is lifestyle to you? _____
On a scale of 1-10, how important is autonomy and freedom to you?
_____
On a scale of 1-10, how important is travel to you? _____
On a scale of 1-10, how important is upside and scalability to you?
_____
On a scale of 1-10, how important is happiness and peace of mind to you? _____

LET'S FIND OUT HOW YOUR CURRENT VEHICLE
MATCHES UP TO YOUR SCORES ABOVE.

Does your current vehicle allow you to make the money you want?

_____

Does your current vehicle allow you to create a lifestyle that inspires
you? _____

Does your current vehicle allow you to create autonomy and freedom?

_____

Does your current vehicle allow you to travel on your terms? _____

Does your current vehicle have endless upside and potential
scalability? _____

Does your current vehicle give you happiness and peace of mind?

_____

If upside, scalability, and income are important to you, then ask yourself: does my current vehicle have the potential to scale me past 7-8?
Yes or No?

Will what you're doing now keep you fascinated and engaged for the
next five+ years?
Yes or No?

Are you in the right business to match your values and needs?
Yes or No?

If you answered NO to the above questions: it might be time for a
new vehicle. I recommend you read the next chapter, where I share my
ultimate 9-to-5 escape plan. It lays out my six proven steps for making your transition as smooth and effective as possible. The goal is to
maximize where you are now and then schedule a definitive date to
leave your current position. Take however long you need to do this, but
don't procrastinate and put it off. This is your life, and if you don't take
action in the present, the future of your dreams will never come.

I left direct sales because I knew that regardless of how many hours I
worked, even if it was over a hundred hours per week, logically, I'd never
make it to the seven-figure mark. The magnitude of my mission was
growing, but my influence and income were capped. The job was exactly

what I needed at the time to build a solid foundation, but I outgrew it. Living incongruently is a major cause of stress and frustration, which is why this rule is so important to building a World-Class life.

If you answered YES to the above questions: continue mastering your craft, exceeding customer expectations, and building a World-Class lifestyle for you and your family. I've added some questions below that delve deeper into the "why" behind your business so we can ensure you're on the path to complete clarity. Be honest and take your time with these. Remember, the only way to change your reality is to deal in reality.

The questions below will only make sense if you run your own business and you're already an entrepreneur. If you aren't, then knowing the answers to these questions will give you a massive competitive advantage when you become your own boss.

Why did you originally get into your current industry or business?

_____

_____

Why are you in it now?

_____

_____

What do you need to get out of this business to stay engaged and fulfilled for the long-term?

_____

_____

How is your business currently doing?

_____

_____

How is the cash flow doing?

_____

_____

What was your gross revenue within the last twelve months?

_____

What was your net revenue within the last twelve months?

_____

How many customers and/or clients do you currently have?

_____

How much are your monthly fixed business expenses?

_____

What are your current personal expenses?

_____

Are you making sure every dollar is spent wisely?

_____

What's the number-one thing that would move the needle for your business in the next twelve months?

_____

_____

On a scale of 1-10, how committed are you to making that happen?

_____

If your commitment level isn't a 10, what needs to change for that to become a 10?

_____

_____

Are you doing what you're best at in your work?

_____

_____

Who do you need in your business? Who needs to go?

_____

_____

Who is your ideal client? Is that who your ideal client should be?

_____

_____

Who would you serve best?

_____

_____

What do you want to see happen at the end of this journey? What's your ideal outcome in the next twenty to thirty years?

_____

_____

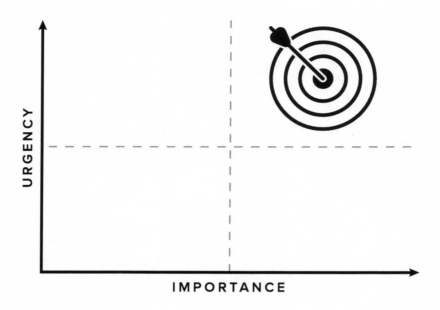

Once you clarify the big picture vision, it becomes much easier to map out your goals.

What do you need to accomplish each quarter to hit your annual goals?

_____

_____

What do you need to accomplish this month? This week? Today?

_____

_____

If you don't know the answers to these questions, discovering the answers should be your first priority. This isn't easy, but it's necessary.

CREATING YOUR WORKFLOW

In addition to clearly defining your goals, it's also important to have a solid workflow in place. If you're unfamiliar with this term, a workflow is essentially a streamlined and automated business task that helps minimize room for errors and increases overall efficiency. It can also help you make quicker, smarter business decisions and allows for more productive collaboration among your team members.

Developing a workflow for your business can be a challenging task, as it requires you to see the big picture while also paying attention to the smaller details that go into it. However, as a business owner, CEO, and entrepreneur, you must develop strategies that help your business grow and stand out in a crowded market. As a result, you'll have the ability to view, operate, manage, and improve your business in drastic ways.

When creating your workflow, it's important to customize it based on where you are currently and what you're trying to accomplish. This will be different for every individual and requires you to pay close attention to your progress and adjust when necessary. Every decision you make throughout the day should be intentional. If you find yourself performing an activity that wasn't part of your agenda for the day, ask yourself why you're doing it and whether or not it should be a priority. Rather than allowing your day to slide off course, stop yourself in the moment and course-correct. It's never too late to save your day from distraction.

The workflow helps you to create and implement an "in the zone" ritual for whenever you might get off track or feel stressed. Your workflow can be the determining factor between earning six or seven figures. The more you focus on using your twenty-four-hour day efficiently, the more cash flow you'll see.

Remember, it's not just about taking action; it's about taking the right action at the right time and making sure the action will give you the best return on investment. To start building your own workflow, answer the questions below:

What time do you start your workday? _____
What time do you end your workday? _____
How many days per week are you working?_____
In a typical workday, how many hours would you say are spent doing something productive for your business? _____

What is holding you back from being more effective and productive?

_____

_____

What are the top weaknesses or issues you need to overcome to be more productive?

_____

_____

Where are your inefficiencies?

_____

_____

What are your most common distractions, and how can you eliminate them?

_____

_____

Describe and visualize your perfect workday.

_____

_____

Having a clear picture of your end goal is critical to success, but it's also important to be present and fully intentional in your day-to-day work. It's not necessarily self-discipline that drives you to success; the habits you create and employ throughout your journey will. Keep pushing forward, keep strengthening your confidence, and most importantly, focus on mastery versus overload. Some of the biggest, most successful businesses in the world do very simple things, but they do them very well. Build a business that is simple, solves a real problem, and will keep you engaged long-term.

Ready to take your business to the next level? Use the execution plan on the following page to define your goals.

EXECUTION PLAN

We covered a lot of different topics in this chapter, and you might be feeling a bit overwhelmed. That's where this execution plan comes in: it was designed to simplify and combine everything you've learned so you can create clear, actionable goals.

Note: If you have yet to finish the questions from earlier in this chapter, I encourage you to go back and answer them before moving on to these. My goal is to help you achieve complete and total clarity by the end of this book, or even by the end of this chapter, but it's up to you to put in the effort.

Are you in the right vehicle? One that matches your values and will keep you fascinated and engaged for the next three to five years? _____
What are the consequences of staying in a vehicle that doesn't match your values or give you long-term fulfillment? Fast-forward five years. Fast-forward twenty years. What would your life look like?

_____

_____

_____

If you are in the right vehicle, what are three ways to improve your results and grow at a faster rate?

_____

_____

_____

What was your biggest breakthrough or perspective shift when assessing your current business?

_____

_____

_____

What one to two actions must be taken for you to reach the seven-figure mark in your business?

_____

_____

Describe your ideal workflow, as well as your ideal day.

_____

_____

_____

_____

_____

_____

CHAPTER 8

THE ULTIMATE 9-TO-5 ESCAPE PLAN

THE SIX PROVEN STEPS THAT MAKE TRANSITIONING TO ENTREPRENEURSHIP A LOT EASIER

IS THE TYPICAL 9-TO-5 JOB ON ITS DEATHBED?

It may be time to rethink the mainstream workday that makes so many people miserable. In fact, the traditional 9-to-5 schedule may already be on its way out. A study examining work-life structures found the concept of a regular eight-hour shift is in decline, with one in five "office" workers now working remotely each week. In fact, more than half (57 percent) of modern American office workers now have the ability to work remotely if they choose to.[4]

I believe this is a step in the right direction. Think of all the negative phrases we use to describe our work and careers, from "the daily grind" to "the afternoon slump." Or the way we talk about the workweek itself?

---

4   Swns. "The Traditional 9-5 Office Job Is Dying." New York Post, *New York Post*, 18 Oct. 2018, www.nypost.com/2018/10/18/the-traditional-9-5-office-job-is-dying/.

"Everybody hates Mondays," "Wednesday is hump day," or the infamous, "thank God it's Friday."

As employees become increasingly frustrated with the traditional workday, we're realizing this outdated system can be reimagined. And it probably should be. The modern 9-to-5, eight-hour workday was invented by American labor unions in the 1800s and was made mainstream by Henry Ford in the 1920s. Workers today accept the same shifts because we're so accustomed to it.

People are breaking the mold and realizing they have options now. The most common questions people ask me because of my previous book, *6 Months to 6 Figures* are, "What's the best way to transition into entrepreneurship," and "What's the best way to transition out of my current job?"

I feel these questions are worth answering, considering the number one regret of people on their deathbed is that they settled for what others expected of them. They were never brave enough to pursue their own dreams, and when they look back at their lives, their unreached goals and aspirations stand out the most. They are often haunted by the decisions that resulted in the life they "ended up with," instead of the life they could have created purposely. The likelihood of regret drastically increases when you try to fit in and conform to others' expectations of you. The older you get, the more expensive the lessons become, and the less time you have to act on your potential. No more settling.

Like we mentioned in the previous chapter, 76 percent of people right now are actively disengaged and don't like what they do. There are even more stats that solidify the extinction of the 9-to-5. For example, 87 percent of people have no passion for their jobs. This means that out of a hundred human beings in the workforce, eighty-seven of them have no passion.

Forbes also states that, on average, people spend 90,000 plus hours of their lives at work and over a hundred hours on their commute alone. That's more than one-third of your life. So, eighty-seven out of a hundred people spend more than one-third of their life with no passion! On top of that, work is the number one factor that influences our personal lives.

Eighty-three percent of US workers suffer from work-related stress.

US businesses lose up to $300 billion yearly as a result of workplace stress.

Stress causes about one million people to miss work every day.

Work-related stress causes 120,000 deaths and results in $190 billion in healthcare costs each year.

Now, some jobs are great, and they're perfect for the people who do them. Some people have their dream jobs, and this is not to downplay those jobs at all. I'm simply saying you were put on this earth to express your creative genius, use your unique abilities, and maximize your potential. There are certain jobs that won't permit you to create a seven-figure income or to truly build a life and business on your terms, and I want to create proper expectations before you take any further action. I couldn't get to a seven-figure income doing the same things that got me to six figures. I needed to develop a different way of thinking and follow a different set of rules. Here are a few questions you must ask yourself to get positioned to make your first six figures, and eventually, a seven-figure income.

- Are there people in my same field or position who currently make a six- or seven-figure income? How long have they been there?
- Do I have the capability to do it faster than the people above?
- Is my income capped, or do I have the capability to make as much as I'd like?
- What do the advancement opportunities look like?
- Can I create more freedom and flexibility if I become more productive and valuable?

If you hate your current position, or it doesn't play to your talents and gifts and you're trying to figure out what's next for you, answering these questions will help. You must answer these questions to gauge how committed you really are.

- How often have you thought about quitting?
- How serious are you about building your dreams?

- How serious are you about living an exceptional lifestyle?
- How serious are you about creating your first seven-figure income?

I started thinking about why more people haven't become entrepreneurs or why people get into the secure 9-to-5 job in the first place. Now, if you love your 9-to-5 and value security over freedom, entrepreneurship is not for you. You can skip to the next chapter and learn how to master the most important business skill to skyrocket your current success. If you've recently quit your job without planning for the future, don't stress out. You'll make it through with these steps—your current state is only temporary. No matter what anyone around you says, you did something very courageous, and the world is massively abundant.

Here's why I believe most people get into a 9-to-5 job without understanding how detrimental it can be to their creativity, passion, happiness, lifestyle, and freedom.

1. THEY THINK IT'S THEIR ONLY OPTION.

This is a really common one. While growing up, I used to tell my mom I didn't want to take the 9-to-5 route. Much respect to my mom, but back in the day, she encouraged it and said, "That's how everybody starts." In her defense, entrepreneurship wasn't as popular, and the online world was in its infancy. I had it ingrained in my head that I had to work a 9-to-5 at an early age. I don't think my mom was the only parent who told their kids to go to college and get a secure job. Just to be clear, you don't have to.

2. THEY THINK IT'S EXPECTED OF THEM.

Most people's circle of influence and environment expect and make the 9-to-5 a cultural norm. When something becomes extremely common, and you hear it over and over, it eventually becomes your reality. If the majority of the people around you have a typical 9-to-5, there's a higher chance you'll follow in the same footsteps.

3. THEY'RE UNCERTAIN AND FEARFUL.

What if I start a business and it fails? What if I can't provide for my family? There's risk with entrepreneurship. Starting a business is risky.

Building a side business is risky. Getting a 9-to-5 is also risky because you risk living your whole life with no passion. So, everything's risky. You might as well risk what's best for your future self, your happiness, and your freedom.

So, what's your 9-to-5 escape plan?

Becoming an entrepreneur, working for yourself, and escaping the 9-to-5 is simple. It does require a decision and some sacrifice, but what worthwhile goal doesn't? It's not easy, but it's *simple* when you have the right roadmap and the right network. It will be challenging and confusing without a plan or any guidance.

THE SIX STEPS BROKEN DOWN

Step 1: Stack Your Ammunition + Fuel
Step 2: The Strengths + Frustrations Formula
Step 3: Increase Your Certainty w/Due Diligence and Network
Step 4: Write Down a Definite DATE
Step 5: Get the Best Training, Mentorship, and Guidance
Step 6: Get a Small Win and Build Some Momentum

STEP 1: STACK YOUR AMMUNITION + FUEL

What is your big why + fifty reasons?

Why do you want to leave your 9-to-5? Why do you want to start a business? Why do you want to become an entrepreneur? Why do you want to be your own boss? Why do you want more freedom and flexibility?

> **Everything starts with "why" and then works its way out from there. If the "why" is strong enough, the "how" will reveal itself.**

So, you need to figure out your top fifty reasons, both internal and external. You need to figure out what has frustrated you in the past. You need to figure out why you don't like what you do or why you have that nagging pull inside of you to do something different. Top performers always have internal reasons layered underneath their external reasons. These reasons should give you juice when you examine them. Not every reason will charge you emotionally, but your goal is to figure out the most compelling and meaningful ones.

If you're not waking up at four or five in the morning, fired up and excited to take on the day, you don't have strong enough reasons. Narrow your top fifty reasons down to your top ten. Write down fifty, and then cross out the ones that aren't internal and give you desire, motivation, and hunger. The top ten reasons should give you chills and fire you up as to why you want to transition out of your 9-to-5. Figure out your "why" and stack so much fuel into those reasons that you don't give yourself any other options.

STEP 2: THE STRENGTHS + FRUSTRATIONS FORMULA

When I transitioned to full-time entrepreneurship, it happened relatively quickly and effortlessly. Why? Because I knew some of the strengths that allowed me to perform well in my previous role would also benefit me in my new career as an entrepreneur.

Strengths are the skills and abilities that come easy for you. When you leverage those skills and abilities, you perform at a higher level. Knowing your strengths means you know the activities that allow you to shine. We'll talk a lot more about how to find your strengths in the next chapter, but let's start with a few questions to get you warmed up.

Identify your strengths:
What are you really good at?
What do you love doing?
What's your unique ability? What would you do for free?
What industries could you see yourself in?
What would keep you engaged and excited for the next couple of years?

Maybe you're a people person. Maybe you're analytical, and you love numbers. Maybe you're good at building relationships and connecting with others. Once you start to build confidence in your abilities, it's important to remember what's frustrated you in the past. There's motivation in pain.

Identify your frustrations:
What are a couple of specific instances or situations you've been in that have frustrated you in the past?
Why did you get so frustrated?
How often are you frustrated?
What are the reasons you don't like your current job?

For me, the answer was simple. I didn't like someone else telling me what I was worth, when to show up, and when I could leave. So, when I had frustrations mixed with strong reasons in a powerful way, there was no other option for me.

Now that you've identified your reasons and frustrations, think of other stories from your past that you can stack up as ammunition and fuel.

STEP 3: INCREASE YOUR CERTAINTY WITH
DUE DILIGENCE AND YOUR NETWORK

Based on my observations, previous conversations, and research, this heads the list as the top reason why people never make the jump to entrepreneurship or quit the job they dislike. They like the certainty of their paycheck coming every two weeks—they haven't created certainty in their *ability* to create their own paycheck. But here's the reality. There is no real certainty in the 9-to-5 anymore. Over 30 million people will lose their jobs because of Artificial Intelligence (AI), and experts say automation could replace 40 percent of jobs in the next fifteen years. Most brick-and-mortars are being forced online, and this is just the beginning. The only certainty one has is their ability to make things happen and their ability to be resourceful. Certainty needs to shift from a 9-to-5 where you're getting paychecks every two weeks to creating certainty in entrepreneurship. How you create your own certainty comes down to two things:

- Due Diligence
- Your Network

The more due diligence you conduct in regard to what industries you want to transition into, the more certainty you create. It doesn't matter if it's sales, entrepreneurship, the speaking industry, becoming an author, or online marketing. The more you can be around people who have already transitioned and are currently making it as an entrepreneur, the more certainty you'll have.

Most people don't want to transition because their certainty lies in their paychecks and their job because everyone else they know also needs that same type of certainty. If you do your due diligence, you'll realize there are a lot of entrepreneurs creating certainty based on their industries, their systems, and their networks. You'll realize you need to get around people who have already transitioned and become entrepreneurs, and that will transform your mindset.

Most people who work a typical 9-to-5 job develop relationships and connections with other people who work the same type of job. If the majority of them are too fearful to make the jump, it will subconsciously affect the others. So, when you do your due diligence, research different industries, and get around people who are making it happen. When you do so, your level of certainty will naturally increase. Do whatever you can to increase your certainty in becoming an entrepreneur.

STEP 4: WRITE DOWN A DEFINITE DATE

I talk to people all the time who have tentative plans to leave their "corporate" job or the job they don't enjoy. I ask them the date they are leaving, and they say they have no idea. The date is what makes it real, and it isn't real until there is a concrete date. If there's no date, you will start to live on "someday island," and always say, "later." "Someday, I'll transition fully. Not right now. Right now, I have bills."

Right now, I just had a kid.
Right now, my kid's five.
Right now, my kid's in high school.

Right now, money is tight.

Right now, I need a steady paycheck.

Right now just isn't the perfect time.

There will never be a perfect time, so it's important for you to create it. As time decreases, intensity, focus, and resourcefulness have to increase. There is a person in our academy who had a respected six-figure salary job. He lives in a small mill town in Canada, and jumping ship to become a full-time entrepreneur was unheard of. He spent almost a year applying these steps, and when he set a date, it became real. Something clicked, and he got into resource mode. He was able to concentrate and zero in on his due diligence and his network. Now, he's fully transitioned and making more than he made as an employee at a corporate job. He's a lot happier and has more freedom because he set a date.

I want you to pull out your calendar and figure out the date you will leave your current position. It won't be easy, but it will be worth it. Embrace the journey and the tough times because that's when your real hunger for success and freedom will develop.

STEP 5: GET THE BEST TRAINING, MENTORSHIP, AND GUIDANCE

Once you set a date, it's important to get the best training, resources, and guidance. Faith is important, but this isn't a time for guessing or wishing. There's no time to waste, and knowing what's coming and what to expect can be a huge advantage—it's the power of anticipation. If you talk with people who play the game at a higher level than you, they can help you identify challenges and opportunities you might not see. This will allow you to move quicker and more strategically. Learning from your own experience is an expensive way to learn, while learning from others is cheaper and more effective.

Studying the best people in chosen industries has unique advantages. Study their stories and their path. I would go as far as to study the traits inside of them that made them want to become full-time entrepreneurs in the first place. Study how they became their own bosses. Study how they became self-sufficient and how they got over their fears.

STEP 6: GET A SMALL WIN AND BUILD SOME MOMENTUM

Momentum is the achievement of small successes consistently, and it's important to get a small win quickly. This could be registering your LLC, attending a networking event, or buying your first course. Getting small results will reinforce the right choices and increase your certainty. With clear goals in mind, it's of great importance to celebrate small wins, as it helps you get closer to achieving the next steps. When you take action and celebrate small victories, you reward yourself for each stepping stone on the way to your ultimate destination.

Time waits for no one, and the new economy requires you to appreciate your value and time at the highest level. It's becoming more commonplace to create your ideal opportunity versus taking what's been given. I know you've thought about quitting your job and living life on your terms, and it's finally time to make it happen. When you make the definite decision, you'll start seeing proof everywhere. Time is going to pass anyway; you might as well work toward something worthwhile.

I was willing to work a hundred hours for myself, so I'd never have to work forty hours for somebody else. Eventually, things changed, and I was able to call the shots and create my own schedule. It'll be an exciting and rewarding day when you finally say goodbye to your 9-to-5 and welcome the new life of complete freedom from an employer. Most people are working just hard enough to not get fired. The big companies know this, and they pay their employees just enough so they don't quit. Don't get caught up in this vicious cycle. I challenge you to follow these transition steps. When you do, I assure you, you'll be able to live a life on your terms, your own way.

CHAPTER 9

RULE 5

WORLD-CLASS BRANDING AND POSITIONING

MORE THAN EVER BEFORE, CONSUMERS HAVE A MULTITUDE OF brands to choose from. Since most of your competitors probably offer similar products and services, you need to truly stand out. You must consistently deliver a positive, memorable experience each and every time your customers think of or interact with your brand.

Branding and positioning are two extremely important marketing concepts for business. While they're both closely related, it's critical to understand the difference between the two and have separate execution strategies for each. In short, branding tells the customer *what* to buy, while positioning tells the customer *why* they should buy it. The results of differentiating yourself in the marketplace may seem obvious, but without understanding the real significance, it's easy to take branding and positioning for granted. In doing so, you'll join thousands of other entrepreneurs who miss this critical component and make the mistake of simply choosing a logo and colors.

Let's delve a bit deeper by reviewing the core components of these two concepts.

BRANDING EXPLAINED

Branding has many components, ranging from the name of a business, to the logo, to the colors used for the website or brand collateral, and so forth. The job of a brand manager is to define the components that are appealing to the businesses' target audience and then get those images in front of the audience as much as possible. Think about Monster Energy (drinks) and its target consumers. They likely aren't stay-at-home moms or retired dads, right? No! They're edgy adrenaline junkies who likely listen to rock music and play video games, and these are the targets of its dark, grungy branding.

Branding is essential for growth and longevity in the new economy. It's what makes the first impression on the target consumer and sets the overall tone for expectations with the product or service. It can also be the most effective and transparent way to distinguish a business from its competition, whether through a memorable logo or a unique, relatable message.

When branding is executed deliberately and strategically, everything becomes more synchronized, which makes it much easier to focus on accurate positioning.

POSITIONING EXPLAINED

Positioning has a variety of components as well but plays a slightly different role in marketing. Branding is primarily about the image of a business, whereas positioning is responsible for the perception of the brand experience. It involves appealing to a target demographic on an emotional level and claiming a reputation or position within its respective market.

Positioning also involves identifying the ways in which your company's offerings differ from those of competitors, whether through quality, affordability, and so forth. For example, let's say both you and your competitor plan to be sponsors at an upcoming event. For that sponsorship to be effective, you need to determine your position in reference to the competition and then define and promote the unique or differing attributes of your brand in an effort to claim the top position.

Now that you understand the difference between branding and positioning, let's explore the benefits of each and how they play a role in your business's growth, income, and overall influence.

THE BENEFITS OF BRANDING AND POSITIONING

After transitioning out of direct sales in 2013, I had some pretty lofty goals as many new entrepreneurs do, with most of them focused on making a massive impact. I wanted to get paid as a speaker, be a guest on the top-performing podcasts, and see my face plastered across *Entrepreneur* and *Forbes* magazines. As naive as these goals seem to me now, I genuinely believed they were achievable at the time and spent months reaching out to my connections, emailing companies, and doing everything I could to make something happen.

The result? Crickets. I couldn't even book a speech for free.

Despite my months of continuous effort, I couldn't move the needle forward. I had to take a step back and analyze where I was going wrong.

Fast-forward to present-day; I've now achieved those initial goals and more. I've been approached by *Forbes* three different times, have a partnership with *Entrepreneur*, and my last twelve to fifteen speeches have been for companies that have reached out to me. I've even had paid partnerships with companies like Marriott, Sony, Bose, Uber, Staples, and many others.

So, what's the key difference between where I started and where I am now?

My focus on positioning and branding.

When you position your brand effectively, you don't have to invest nearly as much money, time, and effort chasing down opportunities. You can spend less time on marketing your brand or testing ideas and more time on delivering to the type of client you want. In fact, that's one of the greatest benefits of effective positioning: rather than chasing, your ideal customers come to you.

HOW TO KNOW IF YOUR BRAND IS EFFECTIVELY POSITIONED

1. Rather than having to find new clients, a consistent stream of customers come to you.
2. You can be selective in who you hire.

3. Your brand essentially markets itself without much investment on your part.
4. Running your business is fairly easy and enjoyable.
5. You've built a raving fan base at a rate quicker than most.

Positioning is about creating a brand people want to be associated with and are therefore willing to pay a premium for, which starts with the brand image. Branding tells the customer what your brand is and helps them decide if it's worth their interest. People should see your label and quickly understand exactly what you do. Think of any major brand you're familiar with—these components are likely all synchronized and evident. You know what they create, who they serve, how they work, and you have a picture of their brand image in your mind. These are signs of a successful brand.

HERE ARE SOME POWERFUL QUESTIONS YOU SHOULD START ASKING YOURSELF

What do you sell?
Is this what your customers want?
What do you *really* sell?

Now, let's ask these questions about a more established brand, like McDonald's.

What does McDonald's sell?

Food? Real Estate? Systems? Opportunity? Jobs? Most people would say food.

I've asked this question on stage, in workshops, masterminds, conference calls, and nobody has ever gotten the correct answer.

What do they *really* sell?

They sell convenience.

Every business and positioning decision they make is based on the convenience of the customer. This is why the documentary *Super Size Me* didn't hurt their sales at all. They have an established, loyal audience that doesn't purchase their product for the health benefits but for the convenience and affordability.

Now let's analyze a business on the opposite end of the spectrum: Louis Vuitton.

What does Louis Vuitton sell?

They sell clothes, purses, belts, and handbags, right? On the surface, yes.

But what do they *really* sell?

They sell an emotion.

When somebody buys Louis Vuitton, they feel a certain way. They don't simply sell material objects; they sell a status symbol. This distinct harmony of positioning and branding has allowed them to build a thriving business with little to no marketing effort. In fact, they welcomed record-high sales in 2018 with a whopping revenue of $53.5 billion, a 10 percent increase from the previous year. How do you create $53.5 billion in sales with no marketing? Through proper positioning, knowing exactly what you sell and who you sell it to.

SHIFT YOUR PERSPECTIVE TO THE NEW ONLINE AGE

While claiming a stake in your desired market won't happen overnight, you can get there much quicker by employing the right mindset. You must wholeheartedly believe in yourself as a business owner and know that, without a doubt, the product or service you're offering is more valuable than the amount you currently charge for it. Bottom line.

This is the first step in this process: shift your perspective.

The likelihood of the marketplace responding because you personally believe people need or want your product is nonexistent. You can't build a brand based on your personal beliefs. You must test the market, understand your audience inside and out, and create a product or service that appeals to *their* personal beliefs.

This also applies to the way in which you present your brand online. One of the top mistakes I see individuals make in the online entrepreneurial space is attempting to sell themselves, their expertise, and their accomplishments. This is an outdated, overused method that may have worked ten years ago, but consumers no longer respond to this. When it comes to selling anything online, the focus should be on selling the solution to a problem your audience is currently suffering from. They don't care about where you went to school or how long you've been in business; they care about whether or not you can fix their problem and get results.

Many online entrepreneurs and salespeople are at the bottom of the totem pole because the market is filled with millions of them. However, at the top of the totem pole is the trusted and leading authority: the number one, go-to source. If you want to thrive, you must be elite and exclusive and establish yourself as a trusted leader within your market. For example, there are 1.3 million real estate agents in the US alone. Becoming the go-to agent in your area is a lot more effective than being "just another agent."

You might be wondering, "How do I establish myself in a market when I'm just starting out?"

The answer is to focus on the marketing of the doing, not just the doing. The "doing" is what is involved with delivering a speech, creating a course, selling real estate, and on and on. However, you must focus on the marketing of your actual craft. For example, instead of being just a speaker, you must also become a marketer of your speaking service. There's no dead end with a good marketing system because the right positioning *is* the best marketing system. And as we discussed earlier in this chapter, the right positioning means having a consistent flow of high-paying customers, clients, and contracts and having ultimate leverage.

Good positioning also means building a sustainable business with a strong foundation versus one that's quickly built on sand and crumbles the minute a wave rolls in. There are thousands of online businesses that use this quick startup method, and most are out of business in less than a year. Instead of trying for a quick start, focus on learning about your audience. What are their problems and ambitions? Where do they want to go in life? Find out everything you can about them, and then take them where they want to go. You can also use this information to differentiate your business from the competition. If a potential customer asks, "Why should I work with your business rather than a different one," you should be able to provide the answer immediately. Don't focus on the competition—focus on differentiation and the elements of your business that make it exclusive and elite.

BEFORE BUILDING A BRAND

Building a solid brand image starts with due diligence and effective research; it's the only way to build a brand that rises above the noise. I've seen a lot of people attempt to build a brand using their own ideas or opinions rather than proven research, and it rarely ever works. Doing the initial research is necessary as it informs you of the right strategy to pursue, whether it's using colors that appeal to your audience or coming up with a slogan that matches your audience's communication style.

As I was building my brand, my team and I spent a lot of time surveying our target audience, and we did so multiple times. We wanted to understand our audience inside and out from every imaginable angle. Another lesson I learned in this process is that you can't begin the research stage without understanding yourself first. You must have complete clarity on your values, your "why," and your reasons for building the brand.

It's also important to research your competitors, not for the sake of comparison, but to understand their target audience and identify strategies they employ to draw consumers in. Knowing the competition also helps you develop your unique selling proposition and components of your brand that set you apart. If they're pursuing their audience from one angle, what could you do differently to reach that audience on a larger scale?

Before starting the process of building your brand, ask yourself the following:

Why should people choose my brand, my product, or my service versus any and every other option available to them?

The fact of the matter is, the market is oversaturated in nearly every industry, and if you can't clearly articulate why a consumer should choose your business over the competition, then you don't deserve their interest. This starts with figuring out who YOU are at your core and the things that make you unique as an individual. That's the point at which you'll truly be able to inspire on a massive scale—when you're no longer trying to be like someone else. Domino's built a billion-dollar pizza empire on the back of a powerful unique selling proposition (USP): *"Fresh hot pizza delivered in 30 minutes or less, guaranteed."*

Note that Domino's didn't claim to be all things to everybody. They didn't claim to have the best-tasting pizza or the finest ingredients. They also didn't claim to be the cheapest. They focused on one thing customers really wanted: on-time delivery. And, on the strength of this powerful USP, Domino's created a billion-dollar empire.

What makes your business different? What's the number-one thing that makes your business more valuable to consumers versus your competitors? List the top five things that make your business or brand stand out from the competition:

1. _____
2. _____
3. _____
4. _____
5. _____

This list shouldn't include attributes you already employ, such as "I'm honest" or "I'm ethical." It should list the things that make you truly exclusive from the competition.

When I initially started out, I relied heavily on the opinions of others to build my brand, and all it did was cause confusion and frustration. I wasn't able to grow and couldn't figure out why. Now that I have some experience under my belt, I understand the importance of authenticity, and I know consumers can see through a false persona much more than we realize.

This isn't to say you shouldn't use inspiration from other brands when building your own. In fact, I always recommend studying elements of other top brands in your market so you can identify consistencies and give yourself a reliable starting point. This is a logical shortcut in the brainstorming process, as well as a foolproof strategy that nearly all new companies employ. Think about it: if a brand has risen to the top of the industry you plan to launch in, then their branding has been proven to work. So, why not use a few of those proven elements for your own brand?

As important as imagery is for a brand, messaging is equally, if not more important. You must understand how your audience communicates and create messaging that appeals to them, which relies on conducting initial research. Look up potential brand ambassadors (individuals likely to adopt your service or product) and identify their communication style, the platforms they use, and the frequency at which they use them. Then, build a messaging strategy focused around those findings.

ESTABLISH A TIMELINE

Once you've gone through the initial research stage, the next step is to create a realistic timeline for the build and launch of your brand. Consider how long it might take to decide on a logo or brand colors and the time needed for development, and then set a logical deadline for each task. This shouldn't necessarily be a rushed process, as it's important to have a brand you're excited about, but don't let yourself get caught up in the web of perfectionism. A brand image is something that should shift with the changing standards of the time, so what you start with likely isn't what you'll end up with.

Now that we've covered the core components of building your brand and establishing your position in the market, let's move on to the next phase of development: building a raving fan base. A tribe. A movement. A loyal following.

BUILDING A RAVING FAN BASE

I'm going to ask a very general question, and I want you to reflect on it for a minute:

What is the purpose of your business?

There are many different answers to this question, but there's one that peaks in accuracy at its core:

> **The purpose of your business is to create loyal and raving fans.**

If you were to ask any organization what their number-one goal is, most would likely say "to get more customers." And how do you get more customers? By creating brand loyalty. Simply put, business is the ability to get and keep customers.

Many businesses fail due to the investment and time commitments required to build a solid fan base. It could even boil down to the business owner lacking social skills. Whatever the reason, I can tell you from personal experience that creating a raving fan base is one of the most effective ways to take your business to an entirely new level and can end up being your greatest asset in the long-term. A business can't function without customers, and a *thriving* business can't function without loyal fans.

Back in 2012, I paid $10,000 to attend a business seminar, which was the most I'd ever paid for one up to that point. I didn't know if any game-changing opportunities would come out of it, but I did know a massive amount of my target audience would be there, and I'd be able to spend the weekend making personal connections with more potential customers than I typically reached in a month. For me, that was enough to justify the investment. I ended up leaving with more connections than I had gained in the full previous year, some of which are still raving fans of my brand to this day.

Aside from the validation it provides, having a raving fan base can offer tremendous benefits for your business both now and in the future. A few of those include:

- **Credibility:** The more people you have talking about your brand, the more credibility you build.
- **Trust:** Consumers are more likely to trust a product or service if they see that other consumers trust it as well.
- **Free Promotion:** If you have enough fans sharing and promoting your product, you don't have to invest quite as much in marketing and promotion.
- **Support:** Having loyal fans means you've connected with the consumer on a personal level, and those consumers share their appreciation by offering support and loyalty when you need it most. This is why musicians like Kanye West can say outrageously controversial things yet maintain consistently high sales. He's built a loyal following who supports his word regardless of what the majority thinks or says.

SO HOW DO YOU START BUILDING YOUR FAN BASE?

It all starts with transformation: you must transform the quality of the consumer's life by providing some sort of value system. This means not only anticipating their needs, but also their wants, whether that's personalized communication, exclusive prices, or next-level quality. Ultimately, you must learn to love your customer more than you love your product because, really, your product wouldn't exist without them.

I've heard so many entrepreneurs rattle on endlessly about the benefits and features of their product, yet they have no idea who their customers actually are. This is an unsuitable business model, and it won't hold up in the new economy as there's simply too much competition. The only foolproof way to rise above the noise is to have a passion for your customer that exceeds that of any other business in the market. After all, why should you receive a consumer's attention and loyalty if you're not willing to offer it yourself?

Shifting my focus to the customer has been one of the biggest contributors to the success of my business. My audience knows I love and respect them because I make an effort to show it on a regular basis. And in return, they not only purchase my products but share them with their network, resulting in a domino effect of promotion and growth.

Your customers are marketing geniuses. They know exactly what they want, and it's your job to find out what it is. Find ways to phone, email, survey, or talk with them about their needs, wants, desires, passions, concerns, etc. People deal with you because they want you to change their life, and it's on you to deliver their wants and needs.

Going forward, I want you to ask yourself the following with every decision you make:

Will this help me create a raving fan base?

This is the question that really got me in the mindset of putting the customer first. It helped me realize that it's not about "me" or what I personally want; it's about "them." It's about the customers who have the potential to become my raving fans.

"There is only one boss. The customer. And he can fire everybody in the company from the chairman on down, simply by spending his money somewhere else."

—Sam Walton, Founder of Walmart

Another thing to keep in mind when building your fan base is that it doesn't have to be a massive number of people—it just needs to be a solid group of extremely devoted individuals. Contrary to popular opinion, you don't need a large audience to thrive. I've realized through my own personal experience and a lot of trial and error you only need 1,000 people to LOVE what you do and be willing to pay for it. The 1,000 fan philosophy has numerous variations online, but all come to the same conclusion. A creator, such as an artist, musician, photographer, craftsperson, performer, speaker, designer, video maker, or author—anyone who produces art or a product or service—only needs to acquire 1,000 raving fans to make a living. Your raving fans will buy most, if not all of what you offer and, in conjunction with lesser fans making sporadic purchases, create a steady and predictable level of income. Your raving fans will spread the word about you, serve as your ambassadors, and cultivate other fans. Business is the management of promises. You must consistently deliver or exceed the promises you make to all your customers.

Creating raving fans doesn't happen overnight, and you won't get them by sharing a couple of inspirational articles. There's a process you

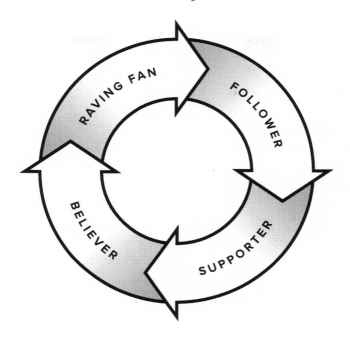

must go through, which requires consistency, focus, and dedication.

I've broken it down into four simple steps:

1. Create followers
2. Turn followers into supporters
3. Turn supporters into believers
4. Turn believers into raving fans

Create followers: Post and promote content, share something motivational, share an article, tweet some great tips, or share interesting information people will enjoy on a consistent, regular basis. This is more surface level, and people rarely turn to true followers or supporters if you just share content.

Turn followers into supporters: Hone in on content with the highest engagement rates and focus your promotions there. This shows your followers you have their best interests in mind, and you will continue to provide them with value that matches their interests.

Turn supporters into believers: Through consistent messaging, value, and connection, you'll start to establish trust with your supporters, and they'll recognize you as the real, authentic deal. They'll see you have authority in the marketplace and will want to be publicly associated with your brand.

Turn believers into raving fans: This happens when your believers are able to reach a goal or fulfill a need due to your efforts, whether it's losing five pounds, increasing their bottom line, improving their relationships, etc. Once you give somebody an actual tangible result, they become raving fans. If you can improve their life in some way, you'll create a raving fan for the long haul.

Once I conceptualized the importance of these principles, I started to base everything around them. People care about what your business can do for them. How will it help them? What's in it for them? Will it solve their problem? Will it make their life easier? Save them money? Educate them? Make them feel something?

Need something more concrete? No problem.

If you can help one million people:

1. Feel better
2. Solve a problem
3. Get educated
4. Look better (health, nutrition, clothing, makeup)
5. Feel secure (housing, safety, health)
6. Feel a positive emotion (love, happiness, laughter, self-confidence)
7. Satisfy their appetites (food)
8. Make something easier
9. Enhance their dreams and inspire hope
10. Then I guarantee you will be worth millions.

So, the next time you're online looking to make money, sit back and ask yourself, "What do I have to offer the world?" If you can offer value to the world, you'll become a magnet for money. One of the biggest mistakes people make in the online world is asking for money and expecting profits without adding any real value or creating raving fans first.

THE SIX STRATEGIES FOR CREATING RAVING FANS

I've learned some great strategies for creating raving fans and a loyal tribe. Here are the ones I've seen with the best results.

Give more than you promote. ALWAYS. Your goal is a 3:1 or 4:1 ratio of giving to promoting. Become known for giving better free content than what most charge for. Before you can focus on profit maximization, you must focus on audience expansion. The best way to extend your audience and fan base is by adding value. Give your best content away. This forces you to level-up and create even better content.

Always leave your clients in a better place and state than when they started. Do everything in your power to help them get the result they are after with your product. Every person in your organization has an impact on outstanding client support and service—from reception to the mailroom to the CEO. You must create a culture where people are passionate about meeting the client's needs.

Run your business in an open, transparent way. When you make offers, be totally clear about what it means to your clients. If something goes awry, tell your clients what happened. In times of uncertainty or stress, you must overcommunicate with your clients and customers.

Always reward your best clients. Give them special benefits, discounts, offers, and value in addition to (or in advance of) what your core clients receive. You need to provide incredible service to create clients for life who will promote you and become your advocates. It's so much more expensive to get new customers than it is to take care of the ones you have.

Create a structure and system focused on client needs. It all starts with this concept. You can create a document that defines your organizational structure and how it relates to client service. You can put a monthly meeting in place with your key employees or partners to remind everyone what the purpose of your business is. You can create a list of top customers and make sure you reach out consistently.

Give back however you can. Give back to your customers, the industry, and society as a whole. If you charge $50k to speak, it's important to do a charity event or speak for free sometimes. I've turned down paying speaking gigs to speak to inner-city kids in the Los Angeles and Newark, NJ areas instead.

You have a huge responsibility as the leader in your industry, city, state, and world to get your product or message out there. We've gone over many ways you can position yourself in the marketplace to attract the right people to your business. Now let's simplify.

EXECUTION PLAN

What can you do to improve the branding and positioning of your current business?

_____

_____

_____

_____

_____

_____

What business are you really in?

_____

What business do you need to be in if you want to see a 5x increase in your results and revenue?

_____

Once again, write out what makes your business different from the others in your industry.

1. _____
2. _____
3. _____
4. _____
5. _____

What are some ideas as to how you can create raving fans in your business? Look at the five factors above and figure out which ones will make the biggest difference in your business.

_____

_____

_____

_____

_____

What does your product/services promise to your potential customers and clients?

_____

_____

_____

_____

_____

RULE 6

WORLD-CLASS HEALTH, ENERGY, AND PEACE OF MIND

> **What if you had all the time, money, and freedom you desired, but NO energy?**

HEALTH IS A VERY UNCOMFORTABLE TOPIC FOR UNHEALTHY PEOPLE.

I have a long family history of health issues. In fact, since I started writing this book, I've learned of multiple family members who have fallen ill, and two of them have now passed away. The worst part is these illnesses and fatalities could have been prevented.

When I've tried speaking to my family members about their poor health habits, I often hear the response, "When it's your time, it's your time." But really, how selfish is that? What if "your time" could be extended by years and therefore prevent massive grief and loss for your loved ones? What if "your time" could be extended so your loved ones can enjoy more time with you? What if it was just a matter of taking responsibility, making tough choices, and making small daily changes? It's really that simple. In hindsight, had my family members done this, they could have spent more time with their loved ones. They could have seen their grandkids, maximized their experiences, and died knowing they had the courage to make true, effective changes in their lives.

This is the dilemma of maintaining or managing health: it's hard work. Not just physically, but mentally. It's something I'm extremely passionate about, and when people neglect their health, I often feel deep rage within my bones. Even as I'm writing this, I can feel the intensity rising in my nerves. Why do I feel so strongly about this particular subject? Why do I get so angry when I see people ignore their health or wait until their back is against the wall to make changes? Why do I feel the need to dedicate an entire chapter to health when this book is supposed to be about entrepreneurship?

I've never publicly expressed an opinion on this topic, and while I feel nervous about including it in the book, I also know this book isn't about me; it's about you. It's about creating awareness, education, and inspiration for those looking to change. If there's anything I want you to get out of this book, it's newly developed confidence in your capabilities, along with the awareness that you have full control over making changes in your life, including your health habits.

On the contrary, I'm also aware your end results are beyond my control. We will each make decisions we deem necessary in our lives. I know because I experienced it with my dad. He's been an alcoholic for as long as I can remember, and his health is now worse than it's ever been. It took me most of my life to realize no matter how hard I try, I can't change him. While that's been difficult to accept, it's also spawned a newfound sense of peace within me, allowing me to focus more on my own health and personal responsibilities. It's also allowed me to enjoy time with my dad and focus more on the good memories we've made.

For the longest time, I felt like I let myself and my family down by not doing all I could to help change his situation, especially being in the business of helping people. At some point, my mom's words, "he has to help himself," clicked, and a sense of peace grew within me. I only met my grandpa on my dad's side once before he passed at the age of fifty-four, and when I think of my kids not knowing their grandpa because of his poor health choices, it saddens me, but it's something I have to accept.

So, while I truly want the best for you, bear in mind this book is not the end-all-be-all. *You are.* You're the one who creates your own path. According to fortune.com, neutrino.com, and medicalnewstoday.com, 90 to 95 percent of cancer cases are caused by lifestyle and environment. This isn't an easy statistic to read, as it ultimately puts the responsibility on us and removes our ability to blame uncontrollable circumstances, whether it be bad luck or genetic causes. After all, the last thing anyone wants to hear when they're sick is that it's their own fault. While some diseases are hereditary, bad health is often born out of unhealthy choices and behaviors.

Now, please keep in mind what I've said in previous chapters:

1. The only way to change your reality is to first deal in reality.
2. The moment you take responsibility for everything in your life is the moment you can start to change anything in your life.

In the end, truth always wins.

WHAT'S YOUR APPROACH TO HEALTH?

I've been obsessed with my health since I started focusing on it in 2009, around the same time I started my business. I started researching lifestyle habits, various diets, and anything that could help me produce natural energy. It was through this process I started to realize a very simple truth: the subject of health is extremely broad and changes on a nearly daily basis. There are documentaries about the vitamins we should take, as well as the ones we shouldn't, and there are thousands upon thousands of blog articles telling us about new, innovative dieting techniques. There are even entire podcasts dedicated solely to portion control. The endless list of resources becomes confusing and overwhelming to consume.

So, who actually has the best approach?

Is it really possible to have this many "experts" on the subject of health?

We may not have the answers to all of these questions, but we do know we're all made up of unique DNA and therefore respond to various health tactics differently. There can't really be a single "best" approach. It's just a matter of finding one that resonates with you on a personal level.

My personal approach has always been a mix of experience and trial and error. I've recently adopted a philosophy similar to Jay-Z and Beyoncé. In the introduction to the book, *The Greenprint*, by Marco Borges, they write:

> "Having children has changed our life more than anything else. We used to think of health as a diet—some worked for us, some didn't. Once we looked at health as the truth, instead of a diet, it became a mission for us to share that truth and lifestyle with as many people as possible...We all have a responsibility to stand up for our health and the health of the planet. Let's take this stand together. Let's spread the truth. Let's make this mission a movement."

They don't trust random documentaries, books, articles, interviews, or opinions when it comes to their health. They trust the truth and do thorough due diligence before making any decisions. That's what I want for my family and myself.

So, how important is health? The answer to this question is best received by individuals who have lost theirs. I've met sixty-, seventy-, and 80-year-olds who claim their biggest regret is allowing their health to deteriorate, and they'd give every single penny they have to get it back. That's the scary thing—you often can't get it back. All you can do is make the right decisions in the moment and continue to do so every day.

HEALTH = ENERGY

One of the biggest advantages of proper health is being able to generate natural energy, which is essential for developing a World-Class life. Having energy gives you a competitive advantage and can set you far above the curve.

Imagine waking up every day and being at peak performance within minutes.

Imagine getting through your entire day without experiencing a crash.

Imagine feeling vibrant and alive daily and having the energy to do and become more.

Energy can significantly impact your business, and I've seen and experienced it firsthand. Nearly every successful person I've met has an unbelievable level of energy, derived from their focus on health, mixed with loving what they do. This not only makes them more optimistic and motivating to others but also much more resourceful. They're always ready to hop on the next opportunity without the crutch of a crashing stimulant, allowing them to remain focused and present in the moment.

Now, let me ask you a question I'd really like you to sit and reflect on:

WHAT IF YOU HAD ALL THE TIME, MONEY, AND FLEXIBILITY YOU DESIRED, BUT NO ENERGY?

This is a major challenge that most of our society faces now due to the nonstop pace of our world and a refusal to focus on health. We wake up feeling tired, fill our body with sugary food, and then spend the rest of the day trying to pick ourselves up off the floor. We use any motivation we have just trying to get through the day, rather than pursuing our goals.

Energy is the most underrated commodity and one of the most important factors in creating an extraordinary quality of life. In order to take your life to the next level, it's crucial to make a commitment to health.

Admittedly, I wasn't good in this area of my life when I initially started my business. Sure, I made money, but I had no energy and therefore lacked the fuel to get ahead. I searched for every competitive advantage possible until I realized it wasn't a secret hack or business tool I was missing; I was just neglecting my body in a way that prevented me from reaching my true potential and the next level of real results in my business.

This realization was probably one of the biggest game-changing moments of my career. I started putting as much focus on my health and energy as I did on my business and felt an almost immediate difference. I was then able to pass these findings on to my team, and we created an overall culture of excellence that's stuck with us to this day. It became less about numbers or what records we were breaking and more about elevating ourselves to a new level of excellence, both in our business and personal lives. And in doing so, success started to come far easier than we had ever experienced before. In fact, our office became the quickest to hit $1 million in annual sales, while breaking numerous other sales records.

Think about the people you respect the most in mainstream media today. Individuals like Tony Robbins, Elon Musk, Oprah Winfrey, Jackie Chan, Angelina Jolie, Mark Wahlberg, Denzel Washington, Will Smith, Keanu Reeves, Tom Brady, Michael Jordan, and Kobe Bryant. Regardless of the industry, greatness is greatness. And how do you think these individuals reached such extraordinary levels of greatness? Not by relying on stimulants to get through the day, but by having a natural, everflowing source of energy.

I still remember what it was like to be lethargic all the time. To wake up feeling awful and dread the thought of pulling my body out of bed and going to work. As painful as it was at the time, I'm grateful to have gone through it. That constant sense of frustration I had paired with a lack of results is what led me to realize that my issues were far greater than what I saw on a computer screen. Maybe energy was the secret piece I had been missing all along.

While we've covered a lot of important topics throughout this book, I can't fully express just how significant this one is. Your health is anything and everything and is the one thing you have complete control over regardless of financial downfalls, market crashes, or other unforeseen circumstances. It's also the one thing that could be the "make it or break it" factor in your future success.

Before we cover the action portion of this topic, it's important to figure out your personal health and energy habits, so you'll know what action to take going forward. This starts with understanding the three types of lives.

THE THREE TYPES OF LIVES

I. CAGED LIFE

People who live this type of life try to meet the expectations of others. They let others dictate who they are, causing their identities to become trapped in a tight box of impossibility. They base their decisions on what others think versus who they really are or what they really want for themselves. They absorb opinions like a sponge and rarely have original thoughts due to their constant desire to be someone other than themselves. These individuals also tend to settle and repeat the same actions over and over again, regardless of past experiences and/or predictable outcomes.

Steve Jobs hated this type of life and addressed it directly and eloquently in one of his commencement speeches:

> "Your time is limited, so don't waste it living someone else's life. Don't be trapped by dogma, which is living with the results of other people's thinking. Don't let the noise of others' opinions drown out your own inner voice. And most importantly, have the courage to follow your heart and intuition. They somehow already know what you truly want to become. Everything else is secondary."

2. COMFORTABLE LIFE

People who live comfortable lives are complacent and easily satisfied. While they might have a deep desire for more, they get stuck in a web of self-doubt and excuses. They have become comfortable with the status quo and aim to simply exist without a struggle. Most people living a comfortable life haven't thought about their greatest aspirations or dreams for years. They often say things like, "This is good enough," and "I'll travel later." They tend to have a "someday" mentality.

3. CHARGED LIFE

People with charged lives create a life of their own design; they have chosen on their own accord. They are focused on serving and contributing to the world at a high level and base everything on their values and standards rather than their fears or limitations. They have high levels of energy, allowing them to be engaged and present at all times. They are living out their true vision, impacting the masses, and enjoying the variety that life has to offer.

Which type of life do you live?

How long are you going to wait to start living the charged and energized life?

To start, you must consciously choose a new self-image and life and fight to forge it into existence by consistently aligning your thoughts and behaviors. This means having the energy and stamina required to bring your ambitions to reality. Stop focusing on your limitations or what's not possible, and instead, focus on the things that you have the ability to change, including your health. You only have one life, and if you don't have the energy to live it to the fullest, you're simply wasting away.

ENERGY: THE EIGHT TRUTHS

While I wouldn't consider myself an expert on health and energy, I've picked up quite a few tips and tricks throughout my years of research and self-experimentation. This has allowed me to develop what I consider to be my eight truths. These truths consist of habits and psychological mindsets that have resulted in consistent, undeniable change within my life, as well as the lives of others. You may have heard some of these from other health experts, while others are more personal and have never been shared before. They aren't traditional energy-related tips, and many of them you wouldn't associate with an energy explosion, but I've experienced firsthand just how much of an impact they can make.

In reading this section, I want you to rate yourself on a scale of 1-10 for how much you're already implementing each of these truths within your life, with 10 being no room for improvement and 1 being that you've never done it before. In doing so, you'll start to gain clarity on just how close or far you are from achieving World-Class health and energy, as well as the areas that might need more attention.

TRUTH 1: CELEBRATING WEEKLY PROGRESS VS. PERFECTION

Our society has a problem with perfectionism. We're always striving to meet unrealistic expectations we set for ourselves, and then we beat ourselves up when we don't reach them. This is one of the biggest energy-drainers out there, yet also one of the easiest to eradicate. It's just a matter of shifting your focus to what you want rather than what you don't have.

It's simple. If you focus on what you don't want, then you'll get exactly that: what you don't want. And if you continuously focus on your problems, they'll inevitably get bigger. However, if you focus on solutions, those solutions will become clearer. I challenge you to use this mindset in evaluating your current and past progress. Rather than focus on what you haven't accomplished, try focusing on what you HAVE accomplished. Don't think about how far you have to go—think about how far you've come, instead. A simple way to make this mental shift is by implementing gratitude into your daily life. As often as you can, ask yourself the following:

What am I grateful for?
What do I appreciate?
What do I have that other people don't?

If you find yourself struggling to keep up, try writing it down in a journal every night. This is also where you can start to jot down your wins from the previous week, which can be as many or few as you'd like. I personally like to write down my top six wins from the previous week, and I do this regardless of how productive my week actually was. They don't have to be huge wins. They could be as simple as "I remembered to pay my utility bill on time," or "I made a new connection at work."

Once you've written down your wins, the next step involves analyzing the areas where you could have improved your progress and production. This shouldn't be done by dwelling on the past, but rather reflecting on the changes you need to make for the future. You must remove any and all emotion throughout this process and reflect on it as if you're evaluating the progress of someone else.

For example, if you wrote down, "I remembered to pay my utility bill on time," evaluate why it's been such a struggle to remember to pay it in the past and make a note of why you were able to remember last week. What did you do differently? Is there still room for improvement?

Most importantly, celebrate the progress you made yesterday, last week, last month, or even last year. You are not perfect, nor will you be able to completely perfect your progress and execution. However, by methodically analyzing where you've been and the steps that have led you to where you are now, you'll have the energy to get where you want to be that much quicker.

Rate yourself on a scale for how well you currently practice this truth:

——————

What can you do to improve this area of your life and increase your energy?

——————————————————————————————
——————————————————————————————
——————————————————————————————
——————————————————————————————

TRUTH 2: THE DAILY PRIZE FIGHTER ROUTINE

The Prize Fighter Routine is a morning routine that sets you up for a *productive* day, not just an average day.

When I get up early after a full night's rest, I consistently have more energy, which directly impacts my self-worth. You've likely heard about the benefits of having a consistent morning routine, but the Prize Fighter Routine goes beyond that. In essence, it's a simple action that serves as a reminder of how serious you are about your success. It's about taking a stand for what you want and boosting your self-confidence. By consistently doing this every day, you'll not only start to feel better about yourself, but you'll start to feel the energizing effects of having higher self-worth.

There are two outcomes you should aim to accomplish with your Prize Fighter Routine:

1. Starting your day off with a positive mindset. This will help you take on whatever the day throws at you without succumbing to negativity, therefore improving your decision-making and overall work performance.
2. Setting your priorities. To accomplish this outcome, I like to mentally walk through my day and make sure I have a full understanding of what my biggest priorities are. I also like to start with my hardest tasks first.

As Brian Tracy states: "You should eat that frog every morning." This essentially means that if you do the hardest thing at the start of your day (such as eating a frog), then everything else that follows will be a cakewalk.

Now that you know the outcomes to aim for, you can try various morning routines to see which one works best for you. There is no single method for everyone, and it all depends on your personal preference. Some examples of effective morning routines include:

1. Spending the first sixty minutes of your morning focusing on yourself. If you aren't fired up and energized, then you can't help others do great work.
2. Reading inspirational, impactful business books. Make sure what you're reading is 100 percent relevant to your vision and that you're focused on mastery, not overload. When you read something positive, and it sparks your mind, it will fill you with energy.
3. Writing in a journal about how you feel. Write down your goals, commitments, or even what's frustrating you. Just let your mind wander and get it all out.
4. Meditating, praying, sitting in silence, or visualizing. A great app I've been enjoying is Headspace, as it guides you through the process of relaxation in a very simple, easy-to-follow manner. Rewire your thinking through the use of daily success statements.

For example:

"I'm open to receiving all life's riches!"

"Day by day, in every way, I am getting better!"

"I am the leading authority for entrepreneurs, and I was born to do extraordinary things!"

"I was born to change the game and be the best in the world at what I do!"

"I understand that the best in the world NEVER lets anything affect their peace of mind."

"There is no shortage of money, and there are billions of dollars in transactions daily."

"I will create massive energy today and feel exceptional!"

5. Visualizing and working on your attitude. The things you think about impacts your energy level. If you focus on what isn't going right in your life, you'll feel depressed and deflated of any energy. This goes back to expressing gratitude. If you have a tough time thinking about the positives, start jotting down the things you're grateful for in a gratitude journal.
6. Sparking your body through meditation or yoga. When you're physically stronger, you're mentally stronger.
7. Reflecting on the day ahead. These are the three questions I ask myself every morning:
8. What am I excited about? What am I grateful for today? What am I committed to making happen today, no matter what?

One thing to keep in mind with your morning routine is there is no specific time that you need to wake up. It's all based on your body and the times when you work best. I have many successful friends who do their best work from 11 p.m. to 1 a.m. and therefore wake up later in the morning. It all goes back to knowing yourself, your body, and creating a routine based on past experiences. As long as you wake up feeling rejuvenated and excited for the day ahead, you're doing it right.

Once you've completed your morning routine, I recommend using the 60-20-60 principle for starting your workday. This is a method I've been utilizing for a long time, and it does wonders for my productivity and overall stamina. Here's how it works:

- Spend the first 60 minutes of your day working on your most important tasks with no distractions (no phone, email, etc.)
- Take a 20-minute break or have a transition trigger that resets your focus and mindset. By rejuvenating, you'll increase your energy and focus for your next task.
- After your break, go back to the same tasks and spend another 60 minutes, giving them your undivided attention.

I can assure you that you'll get more done in this 2 hour and 20 min period than you would during a normal distraction-filled workday. Though to truly crush this principle, you must plan your day accordingly. Make sure you've considered all the tasks you have on your plate and that you put the hardest or most important ones at the top of the list. It's also crucial to consistently take "disconnect" breaks to refocus your mind, regardless of how "in the zone" you may feel.

By practicing this technique on a daily basis, you'll notice a significant difference in your natural energy production and overall productivity.

Rate yourself on a scale of 1-10 for how well you currently practice this truth: _____

What can you do to improve this area of your life and increase your energy?

_____

_____

_____

_____

TRUTH 3: REDUCE STRESS AND TAKE PROBLEMS HEAD-ON

As many of you likely already know, one of the biggest energy zappers out there is stress. According to Psychologist Paul Baard, PhD, "Stress is the result of anxiety, and anxiety uses up a whole lot of our energy." Similar to worry or fear, Baard claims that stress can leave you mentally and physically exhausted, regardless of how active you were throughout the day. More commonly, he says, "Low but chronic levels of stress erode energy levels, so over time, you find yourself doing less and feeling it more."

While it's important to know how to reduce stress, it's also true that stress isn't always the enemy we make it out to be. In fact, here are some facts about stress that might surprise you:

- Stress helps boost brain power
- Stress makes you more resilient
- Stress motivates you to succeed
- Stress pushes you past your comfort zone

The main problem occurs when we don't take the necessary time to refuel and recover from the stress we endure, whether at work or at home. This causes us to lose all productivity, momentum, and ultimately, energy. Sure, stress might be uncomfortable, but this book isn't about being comfortable; it's about becoming a true Game Changer, which requires that you push past your current limits and learn how to work through challenging, stressful situations. Having a high tolerance for stress and pressure is a skill that successful people are paid very highly for. It can also help you expand your capacity for struggle, therefore enabling you to deal with more, take on more, and become more.

MAIN CAUSES OF STRESS

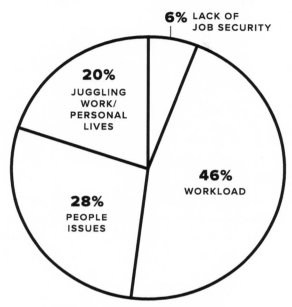

Source: EAP provider ComPsych's first half of 2006 StressPulse Survey

In addition, being able to quickly adapt to stressful situations and refocus your mind can help you stay calm and in control, regardless of the challenges at hand. Have you ever noticed how the world's greatest achievers seem to stay relaxed under massive scrutiny, pressure, or drama? This is because they've learned how to effectively cope and recover from stress. It's also important to not let past grievances or negativity re-enter your brain space and create self-inflicted stress. If it doesn't positively serve you in the present, then you must force yourself to let it go.

In order to effectively recover from stress, it can help to have a go-to routine. Here are a few things I practice to get myself back in the zone after stressful situations:

- Change my environment and shift gears
- Shift my focus and change my perspective
- Analyze why I'm feeling a certain way

- Connect with my mentors or role models
- Focus on heightened awareness and dig deeper

In the introduction module of our Game Changers Academy, we walk our members through a deep-dive exercise that helps them to clear their minds and get in a fresh state to start their workday. I recommend you try it as well:

- Fix or cut off any toxic or strained relationships
- Decrease the time you spend with anybody who isn't sold on YOU and YOUR dreams
- Dismiss, complete, or delegate any project that isn't finished
- Address head-on anything that's been festering in your mind
- When you face your problems head-on, a weight will be lifted off your shoulders, allowing you to be more resourceful, fulfilled, and energized.

Rate yourself on a scale of 1-10 for how well you currently practice this truth: _____
What can you do to improve this area of your life and increase your energy?

_____
_____
_____
_____

TRUTH 4: CREATE AND LIVE IN YOUR OWN REALITY

In order to be a true Game Changer, you must set and follow your own rules. Getting caught up in society's expectations or letting others dictate your self-worth, vision, feelings, or attitude can lead you to feel trapped in a world you didn't create. And the more you try to adhere to the standards of others, the more energy you'll drain. Living in others' reality or constantly trying to fit in and please them takes more energy than you realize.

In order to break this issue, it's important to set strict criteria for what you allow to impact or change your mindset and attitude. If most of society isn't happy and you live by society's rules, what do you think will happen? You'll also become unhappy. This is why it's important to create your own rules to live by and then continuously adapt based on your values and what's most important to YOU and YOUR happiness.

"Whenever you find yourself on the side of the majority, it is time to pause and reflect."

—Mark Twain

It's important you don't blindly follow societal "norms" without thinking twice and creating your own way of living.

While there's nothing wrong with social norms, it's important to remember you don't have to mold your life around them. It's all about doing things on your terms and creating a reality based on what YOU want and value. For example, I work nearly every Sunday and then take a day off during the middle of the week. I've found this schedule works best for me due to the fact that most don't work on Sunday, so I don't have to worry as much about incoming calls or emails. I learned early on in my career that having a full day of uninterrupted work is important for my productivity, so I created a schedule that allows for that.

The expectations or standards of society should never dictate your decisions or actions. It's about what's best for you, your family, your willpower, and your mindset. I'm sure that some of you reading this book have the typical 9-to-5 job, therefore making this concept a bit more challenging to act on. However, even in a typical 9-to-5, there are dozens of ways to differentiate yourself and live life on your own terms.

Rate yourself on a scale of 1-10 for how well you currently practice this truth: _____
What can you do to improve this area of your life and increase your energy?

_____

_____

_____

_____

TRUTH 5. PROTECT YOUR MIND AND BODY ABOVE ALL ELSE

The things you put in your mind determine how you think and what you do. Similarly, what you put in your body determines how you look and how you feel. So, how do you achieve World-Class health? By protecting both.

The extremely successful Dr. Oz was recently asked what his secret was for managing his time. He performs 250 open-heart surgeries each year, is a professor at Columbia University, a chairman of surgery, a medical program director, a prolific writer, makes regular appearances on TV and radio, and he's now launching his own TV show on the Oprah Winfrey Network. Not to mention he's a devoted husband and father of four. His answer to this question was one of the best distinctions about time management I've yet to hear:

"It's not about time management. It's about energy management. That is everything."

The goal is to look for ways to get a better "return on energy" (ROE). If you're doing a good job at efficiently managing your time, but you're spending that time on things that drain you of happiness and joy, are you really doing that much good? A good way to know if something is worth your effort and time is to ask yourself, "Will this give me energy or take it away?"

Rather than doing what you *think* you should do, spend your time on the things that energize you, and guard against anything that depletes it. It's really that simple. The things you choose to do should also be congruent with your goals. For instance, even if going to the movies gives you energy, that likely wouldn't be a good option to help you reach your goals.

Once we understand that time is outside of ourselves and energy is within us, it becomes clear that energy is our currency for living. Successful people understand this at a level that most don't normally think about. It's all about making choices that result in a healthy, energized state of being.

The answer to getting a better ROE lies in the understanding of these three energy sources:

- Physical
- Emotional
- Mental

Physical Energy

There are two primary factors that fall under the category of physical energy: nutrition and exercise.

When it comes to nutrition, we've been led to believe a lot of different things about what's right to consume, how much we should consume, how quickly we should consume, and so forth. But in reality, it's all based on what each of our bodies need individually. I won't go into the scientific details behind proper nutrition, but I do recommend you study up on it yourself and develop a clear understanding of what your body responds to best. Find out what type of food and nourishment will give you the best competitive advantage.

Here are a few of my own nutritional habits you're welcome to try, though they may not work for you. Figure out what YOUR body needs.

- Eat organic, whole foods, and fresh fruits and vegetables
- Practice portion control and never eat to the point of being full (the process of digestion is one of the body's most energy-consuming functions, so the more you eat, the more energy you use).
- Eat small meals multiple times a day and only consume foods that increase energy, such as cucumbers, salads, walnuts, trail mix, parsley, raw spinach, broccoli, celery, garlic, green beans, lima beans, carrots, beets, zucchini, kiwi, avocado, kale, Brussels sprouts, and edamame.
- Drink tons of water
- Drink a green shake in the morning (make sure any green drinks you consume have trace minerals, Echinacea, and ginger).

Nothing tastes as good as healthy feels.

In terms of physical activity, I've found that when I exercise on a regular basis, I have an easier time waking up in the morning, getting things done, and feel far more passionate about my work. This is because the body craves physical activity and doesn't function at peak performance without it. I personally need to work out five days a week to achieve World-Class energy, but it may be different for you. As long as you're sticking to a routine and feeling positive energy-releasing effects, you're doing it right.

For those struggling to get into the habit, I thought I'd share my own personal workout regimen so you can try it out yourself. There are three key components to it:

1. Cardio
2. Weights
3. Stretching

Cardio: Whether it's hiking, running, swimming, biking, or a group activity, I incorporate twenty to thirty minutes of cardio into each of my workouts (or longer if I have yet to break a sweat).

Weights: I love lifting weights as they make me feel stronger—not just physically, but emotionally, too. I typically spend twenty to thirty minutes three times a week focused on weightlifting. I don't want to think about what exercises I need to do or what body groups to work out, which is why I've hired a personal trainer. When I'm not an expert in an area, I delegate to those who know more than me as often as possible.

Stretching: I've recently been practicing yoga, and it's helped me calm my mind and get into a more relaxing and peaceful state. I specifically practice in the mornings after I wake up.

When establishing a workout plan, it's important to start gradually to get your body in the groove of things. Try doing one day a week at first and then build up from there. If you find yourself struggling with accountability, find a trainer or a gym buddy who will help you stay the course. It's all about finding your sweet spot, and once you do, you'll be amazed at how much your life will begin to transform for the better.

Emotional Energy

Having emotional intelligence is one of the most underrated skills. It's also crucial for success in the new economy. In order to perform at our best and generate natural energy, it's important to know how to access and utilize the positive while steering clear of the negative.

THE DRAINING IMPACT OF NEGATIVE ENERGY

If you've ever found yourself feeling exhausted after a fight with a loved one or a bad day at work, you've likely experienced the draining effects of negative energy. For some of you, it could even be a more frequent issue, resulting in a back and forth internal battle at the drop of a hat.

The quality of our energy hugely diminishes over time when we let the bad interfere with the good. In fact, according to experts, the impact of negative energy can become so severe that it can even lead to further health conditions such as chronic tiredness, or Chronic Fatigue Syndrome, and an overall lack of motivation.[5]

The tricky thing about negative energy is that it doesn't always provide us with physical cues that indicate the need for rest. Instead, we become easily agitated, foggy-brained, and stuck in an endless loop of stress and exhaustion without really knowing why. This is why so many of us set out to accomplish a goal with the best of intentions yet fail to follow through—we allow ourselves to be consumed by the various curveballs of life.

What's the trick to beating this silent monster? Is there a solution that doesn't require a significant lifestyle change? Yes! It all starts with improving emotional intelligence and training the brain to use a different lens.

Here are a few brain-altering methods proven to reduce the occurrence of negative thoughts when practiced on a regular basis:

---

5 "Tiredness and Fatigue: Why It Happens and How to Beat It." *Medical News Today*, MediLexicon International, www.medicalnewstoday.com/articles/8877.

1. **Observe your thought patterns.** Whether done through silent reflection or journaling, the goal is to uncover the source behind your negativity and then eradicate it. For instance, is the negative thought based on judgment of yourself or someone else? Are you focusing on your failures? Are you subconsciously comparing yourself to others? Whatever it is, take note of it as soon as it comes up and then actively counter it with two positive observations or things you're grateful for. While it may feel forced at first, it will become a natural, automatic process over time.

2. **Rid yourself of negative influences.** If there's a dark cloud hovering in your life, be it a friend, family member, or daily habit, you must take the necessary action to remove it. This isn't to say you need to ditch your friends or family altogether, but if you find a conversation is taking a negative tone, try to gracefully change the subject to something more positive. If it becomes a recurring theme, then it might be time to remove some of those influences.

3. **Do something kind.** One of the quickest ways to fall into a pit of despair is focusing on our own misfortunes and forgetting about those around us. To counter this, try stepping outside of your daily routine and do something generous or helpful for someone else, ideally once per day. Call a family member or friend in need, carry groceries for a stranger, or help a coworker complete a task. Whatever it is, do it with sincere, genuine effort. You'll be amazed at how quickly those negative thoughts melt away.

Mental Energy

Whereas emotional energy refers to the processing of our feelings, mental energy is responsible for powering our thoughts and ideas, and they often work hand in hand. Our ability to generate and maintain mental energy requires that we have a steady handle on our emotional state due to the impact it can have on our cognitive abilities. For example, being filled with anxiety about an upcoming presentation can cause you to make simple, obvious mistakes that hinder the overall message. On the contrary, being filled with optimism could help you discover new, strategic information, enabling you to better drive your point home.

When it comes to mental energy, it's not just about knowing how to generate it; it's about being able to renew it when necessary. Most of us have faced the dreadful impact of mental burnout. That terrible feeling when you've been on a roll all week, knocking out tasks left and right, then you sit down in front of your screen and randomly draw a blank. It's an unpleasant, frustrating feeling, but it's your brain's way of telling you it's time to either recoup or get a change of scenery. Failing to do so could result in more frustration, increased mistakes, and an even longer, more severe period of burnout.

To improve mental energy, you must treat your mind wisely and put it on a pedestal. Similar to how an athlete trains their muscles, there are methods you can use to ensure your brain functions at peak capacity as well:

- Daily meditation (ten minutes minimum): For most of us, we use the left part of our brain for day-to-day tasks, so it's much more likely to get bogged down than the more creative, intuitive right side. By implementing meditation into your daily routine, you essentially slow down brainwaves and force an internal "reset," which, in turn, helps with mental clarity and problem-solving abilities.
- Brain balancing: This might sound a bit out of the ordinary, but it's actually a very effective way to increase overall brain efficiency. For this exercise, start by closing your eyes and visualizing your brain inside your head. Picture the left and right sides, with the corpus callosum, or centerline, between. Imagine each side is filled with an energy-filled fluid, and that on the left side, the fluid level is higher than on the right. Imagine "poking holes" in the corpus callosum so the energy-fluid can flow from the left side to the right until the two sides are leveled out. Affirm to yourself, "My brain's energy is now balanced, and I am centered."
- Power naps: You've likely experienced the replenishing effects of power naps, but did you know they also increase alertness and improve memory? A ten- to thirty-minute daily nap between the hours of 1 p.m. and 4 p.m. will do wonders for your remaining work-

day. So much, in fact, that many companies have started to install "napping rooms" on-site with the hopes of improving employee productivity.

Rate yourself on a scale of 1-10 for how well you currently practice this truth: _____
What can you do to improve this area of your life and increase your energy?

_____

_____

_____

_____

TRUTH 6: MAKE TIME FOR CREATIVE THINKING

We've all heard the phrase "think outside the box." Whether it's from a teacher, boss, or coworker, it's often used in the context of encouraging creative, unique ideas. However, this phrase fails to consider whether or not there's already a ton of junk inside of the box.

This is the most important component of creative thinking: learning to let go of thoughts that aren't serving you in the moment. You must give yourself permission to stop thinking about any problems or stress in your life and force your thoughts elsewhere. This means letting go of the uncontrollable, refraining from dwelling on the past, and understanding that the future is the only thing that can be changed. In doing so, you'll be able to explore beyond the box's boundaries and access the truly exciting and revolutionary ideas that are often brewing beneath the mundane ones.

Now in terms of getting your mind into the place of creativity, this might come easier for some than for others. We're not all naturally attuned to having creative thoughts ready to be presented at a moment's notice. However, you might be surprised at how easy it is to get your brain into a creative space, regardless of how creative you actually are. Here are a few things to consider when trying to get your creative juices flowing:

1. Our brain thinks more creatively when we're tired. The brain is less likely to filter out distractions when tired, and while that may be detrimental during normal working hours, distraction and wandering thoughts are actually a benefit to creative thinking.

2. Exercise improves creative thinking. We all know exercise is good for us, but did you know it also stimulates the part of the brain responsible for coming up with creative ideas? *Psychology Today* said it best: "Sweat is like WD-40 for your mind—it lubricates the rusty hinges of your brain and makes your thinking more fluid. Exercise allows your conscious mind to access fresh ideas that are buried in the subconscious."

3. Traveling abroad can improve creativity. Think about the last time you submerged yourself in a new environment. You were likely exposed to sights, sounds, and even smells you hadn't experienced before. This exposure aids in the creative process. The more connected you are with the outside world, or even with other cultures, the more you'll be able to access and use your senses within your own creations.

Rate yourself on a scale of 1-10 for how well you currently practice this truth: _____
What can you do to improve this area of your life and increase your energy?

_____
_____
_____
_____

TRUTH 7: THE GAME CHANGERS VACATION RITUAL

We are the sum of our total experiences.

In other words, you could be the founder of the most successful business on the planet, bringing in amounts of money that others can't even fathom, but if you haven't created a lifestyle you're proud of, then none of that matters. You've done it all wrong.

Most people do the same thing, with the same people, in the same way, every day and every week, but the human brain craves excitement. Success doesn't happen by playing it safe. It happens by seeking out new experiences and fueling our desire for the unexpected.

Before I begin every week, I ask myself a very powerful question: What am I excited about this week? If I don't have something to look forward to, I make an effort to create it. This process of creating excitement helps to prevent the days, weeks, and months from stringing together into a long, unending line of complacency. It's also one of the biggest fuelers of natural, recurrent energy.

Start practicing this truth by building an easy-to-follow system for yourself. While it may sound strange to build a system focused around excitement and fun, having a system in place is necessary for creating habitual change, regardless of what that change is. Whether it's setting a certain day of the week aside for a mini-vacation or deciding on a specific time to unplug every day so you can explore a new part of your city, the most important thing is to hold yourself accountable and never let the urgency of life get in the way.

Here are some simple ideas, but I want you to get creative based on your location:

- Watch a movie at a new location
- Try a new food
- Go on a micro-adventure
- Visit museums
- Visit aquariums
- Study design or art
- Read a great book
- Visit the ocean or local lakes
- Try outdoor yoga
- Play a sport
- Have lunch with fun people that you enjoy being around
- Get a massage
- Go to a park or take nature walks
- Do a scavenger hunt

Look up the top things to do in your area and think outside the box. How often are you really exploring new areas? How often are you switching things up? How often are you taking vacations? You don't have to leave the country or take a week off. A vacation could be as simple as taking a two-day road trip to someplace new, a place that invokes true inspiration. According to an article published in *The New York Times*, research indicates that "awe" is an important component of daily life, as it helps us to feel more connected with people and nature and gives us the sense that we are part of something bigger than ourselves. This is especially important in an era where we spend more time staring at our devices than we do connecting with actual human beings. In order to live a fulfilling life, you must break the mold and continuously remind yourself of the wonder that surrounds you.

When executing this truth, keep in mind the significance of being present in your normal, daily routine. When you're with your family, focus on your family. When you're at work, work! The only effective way to take advantage of the Game Changers vacation ritual is to make sure you're as efficient as possible with your time. Failing to do so could mean the difference between having an amazing, awe-inspiring experience or being consumed with how much work you left behind.

Rate yourself on a scale of 1-10 for how well you currently practice this truth: _____
What can you do to improve this area of your life and increase your energy?

_____

_____

_____

_____

TRUTH 8: PERSONAL REJUVENATION AND RENEWAL

No matter how much you fight it, we all need a break sometimes. And in fact, implementing regular breaks (or moments of rejuvenation) is one of the most beneficial things you can do for your career. Even pro athletes understand this truth. They don't spend every waking moment practicing.

The first step in practicing this truth is to change your environment. A break isn't a break if you're still sitting in your office. Mix things up, so the break is truly distraction-free and not part of a normal routine. In addition, make sure to calendar this time and create a system for it. For me, this is every Sunday. I spend fifteen minutes thinking and planning ways to rejuvenate and reset my brain. You must protect this time when it comes, and don't let it be the one task you constantly reschedule or don't have time for. You have a responsibility to yourself, your employees, and your family to ensure that you continue to function in tip-top shape, meaning you must make time to reset.

Elite performers understand they can't run at full speed nonstop. They run their life in cycles. Think about any great athlete; they don't go all out every single day. They work with massage therapists, they take time off to let their muscles heal, they enjoy their family, etc. I used to never take days off and believed that if I wasn't working, my competition was passing me by. That was a six-figure mindset, but if you want to get to a seven-figure mindset, then you have to know the true importance of rejuvenating your mind, body, and spirit. You must achieve a balance of being on your A-game and having days of recovery. There is nothing wrong with stress as it makes you play your best game, but there is a problem when people don't take time to recover from the stress or the activities that caused the stress.

Some best practices and examples to make sure you take the proper time and action to recover are completely unplugging during the break (so you don't get distracted and lose focus of the purpose of the break), getting a massage every week, joining a yoga class, practicing meditation, immersing yourself in nature, taking a mini-vacation, or building in other scheduled breaks and adventures into your schedule.

You only get one body and one mind. Take care of them and turn the engines off to allow yourself to reset.

Rate yourself on a scale of 1-10 for how well you currently practice this truth: _____

What can you do to improve this area of your life and increase your energy?

_____

_____

_____

_____

EXECUTION PLAN

You've already answered a lot of questions throughout this chapter so let's simplify.

Have you placed a big enough emphasis on energy in the past twelve months? _____

If Yes...

Starting this week, what is one action you can take that would improve the quality of your life and energy, taking you to an even higher level?

_____

_____

_____

If No...

Why do you feel you haven't taken your energy seriously in the past twelve months?

Starting this week, what is one action you can take that would improve your quality of life and energy?

_____

_____

_____

Go through all of your answers from this chapter and write down which actions will make the biggest difference in your overall health and well-being, starting right away.

How different would your energy be if you focused on these actions?

_____
_____
_____
_____
_____
_____

CHAPTER 11

THE 7 PROVEN AND POWERFULLY EFFECTIVE PRODUCTIVITY AND PROFIT MAXIMIZERS

"It is not enough to be busy. So are the ants.
The question is: what are we busy about?"
—HENRY DAVID THOREAU

LIVING A PRODUCTIVE LIFE IS ABOUT BEING COMMITTED TO PROGRESS without losing sight of your ideal vision. It's not just about the results you get or how much action you take throughout the day; it's about creating the freedom to be with your loved ones, do what you want, and have 100 percent control over your future. The new economy requires you to respect your time and manage it effectively—those who don't are leaving thousands or potentially millions on the table.

Some people intentionally hide their lack of accomplishment behind the mask of activity and sometimes frantic activity. Others simply can't tell the difference between activity and achievement.

One of the most productive people I've ever studied, Dan Kennedy, states:

> "Defining activity is easy. You see it all around you, and you engage in it pretty much every minute of every day. There can be a lot of people putting in 40 hours a week and even running around while doing it with nothing getting done. Meetings held. Paper moved. Warner Bros. Tasmanian Devils stirring up their own little tornadoes—but when the dust settles, there's nothing to show for it. Defining accomplishment is a bit more difficult because it needs something to be measured against. It requires context."

Being busy is a form of laziness—lazy thinking and indiscriminate action. Being overwhelmed is often as unproductive as doing nothing and is far more unpleasant. A lot of entrepreneurs I know think they can solve big problems just by throwing more hours at them. They try to make up for intellectual laziness with forceful action. This rarely results in solutions. Being selective and taking more intelligent action creates the path to being highly productive. You aren't more productive because you're working all the time. In reality, it's actually the opposite.

Being productive is about using your time as efficiently as possible, whether in your business or when working on tasks at home. For some of you, this might require that you spend extra time planning out your day or reflecting on what was accomplished at the end. However, by utilizing self-discipline and applying some of the productivity-based habits below, working efficiently will eventually become second nature and will enable you to reach World-Class status at a much quicker pace.

PRODUCTIVITY REDEFINED

Productivity: getting the result that you want.

Entrepreneur: someone who builds a profitable business.

Entrepreneurial Productivity: wanting and having the ability to build a business that grows, makes a profit, and gives you increasing income.

Productivity is more than results and getting things done. It's about creating the freedom to be with family, do what you want, and have 100 percent control over your future. Productivity isn't about doing more, faster; it's about doing the right things, deliberately and with intention. Feeling the need to be busy all the time is a trauma response and fear-based distraction from what you'd be forced to acknowledge and feel if you slowed down.

My definition of productivity is: the use of your time, energy, *intelligence*, and resources in a calculated manner to move you measurably closer to meaningful goals.

Much of what I thought productivity meant in the past has been proven wrong. Sometimes the best way to learn a new idea is to first "unlearn" an old idea that's hindering it. Here are some of the biggest perspective shifts I've had to make. These must be understood before strengthening your foundation:

- It's not about the hours you work, but the work you put into those hours.
- It's not about working harder or smarter; it's about working right.
- Being productive doesn't mean getting everything done.
- There are people busier than you who are getting more results with more peace of mind and less stress.
- Focus is more important than intelligence, and focus is ultimately a matter of simplicity and decision.

In 2011, I left my office at around 10 p.m. I was the last one there. I was exhausted and had to get up the next morning at 5:30 for an early meeting. I had the realization I couldn't keep living like that, and something had to change. I told myself that night:

> **"I will be more disciplined instead of working all the time."**

This statement changed my life and forced me to become more intentional in everything I did.

Here are some of my favorite productivity maximizers for you to implement, study, and teach to those you lead. Don't try to put these into practice all at once. Rather, pick and choose the ones you feel would make the biggest difference in your business. Once you see results and they're ingrained in your day-to-day business, then move on to the next one. We will then dive into identifying profit-maximizing activities and nonnegotiable value actions.

These maximizers are designed to help you be more productive in your business, so your business can earn more profit and pay you more income. Consistent income allows you to put systems in place so you can remove yourself from day-to-day operations.

1. GET IN THE ZONE

A "zone" is essentially a state of mind where peak performance and output is reached, and it's what you should aim for every day. You're three times more productive when you're in the zone, and you only get in the zone when all distractions are eliminated. If checking your email throughout the day pulls you out of the zone, set aside a specific time each day to check your email and stick to it. You must create a plan to fight interruptions and commit yourself to it. If you don't have a plan to interrupt your interruptions, your plans will always be interrupted.

2. LIMIT YOUR ACCESS

Teach people how to communicate with you and start limiting your availability. Millionaires understand their time and energy is a privilege. Even if you're not yet at the six-figure mark, you must utilize this strategy for the sake of productivity. I haven't answered calls from random numbers in years, and I keep my phone on silent at all times. As a result, I'm able to accomplish more in an hour of uninterrupted time than most can accomplish in four hours. Take it from me, the more you protect your time, the more valuable it becomes.

3. PUT TIME-LIMITS ON EVERYTHING

It's a proven fact that humans work more efficiently when time restraints are in place, so start setting them. Parkinson's Law dictates that a task will become bigger in importance and complexity in relation to the time allotted for its completion. In other words, if you give your team a month to complete a small project, it will likely become far more complex and unachievable than if you were to give them a week. Time pressure forces us to focus on execution and eliminate nonessentials. It obligates us to be productive and removes the ability to overthink, which makes for a far more productive and pleasant work environment.

4. FOCUS ON GROWTH, NOT MAINTENANCE

In my experience, most things entrepreneurs focus on aren't moving their life or business forward. In fact, most of the things they do in their business don't accelerate growth—they just "maintain" at best. In every business, there are tasks that produce big growth while pushing the business forward, and then there are tasks that simply maintain it. Which ones are you focusing on? Most defer to maintenance-related tasks as they tend to require less thought yet still produce the false sensation of productivity. In reality, however, falling into the hole of maintenance-only work is one of the most counterproductive things you could do for your business. As a rule of thumb, any and all tasks that produce trackable growth should be completed by you, the owner, while all other tasks should be delegated. You've built a business because you have the skills necessary to do so. It's just a matter of being disciplined enough to continuously use them.

Execute the Delegation Rule

If it's not a strength and somebody can do it 80 percent as well as you can, delegate it. You should execute this rule especially if you're busy beyond belief and you're unable to accomplish all tasks on a daily basis.

5. BACK-ON-TRACK RITUALS

It's impossible to stay in the zone 24/7, but seven-figure earners stay in the zone more than the majority. To do this, you must create rituals to draw you to the task at hand when you begin to feel unfocused. Back-on-track rituals are great after a holiday weekend with family, the day after a vacation, or when you're simply not "feelin' it." Just the simple act of admitting that you're unfocused is a big step, but allowing that lack of focus to turn into negative momentum is how complacency occurs. If you're having trouble coming up with a ritual, try a few of these:

- Change your environment.
- Call a mentor or someone playing the game at a higher level.
- Get active and spark your body. Play basketball, go for a jog, or work out.
- Listen to something motivational.
- Take a thirty to sixty-minute break.
- Journal and look at your goals.
- Enjoy nature alone, with no technology.

6. STAY IN YOUR OWN WORLD

Instead of conforming to the social norm, go against the grain and create an ideal workflow based on what's best for you. Only *you* know when you have the most willpower. Too many people let others affect their mental state of mind, as well as how they live. This is why it's important to create your own rules to live by and then continuously adapt based on your values and what's most important to YOU and YOUR happiness. Whenever you find yourself on the side of the majority, it's time to reality-check yourself.

It's 6 a.m. I gotta get up.

It's 5 p.m. I gotta stop working.

It's Friday night. I gotta go out.

It's Sunday. I gotta relax.

It's the holidays. I gotta see family.

I've been working two weeks straight. I gotta take a break.

NO, YOU DON'T.

7. FOCUSING ON THE RIGHT ACTIVITIES

If you are doing something well and it's unimportant, it doesn't make it more important. Activities that aren't connected to an outcome or purpose are the drain of all productivity. Understand that what you do is a lot more important than how you do it. Effectiveness is still important, but it's useless if it isn't applied to the right things. There are a handful of tasks you could focus on to create exceptional outcomes for your goals. It's easy to get caught in a flood of trivial matters, and the key to not feeling rushed is remembering that a lack of time reflects a lack of priorities. Take time to stop and refocus your priorities as often as needed. Intelligent thinking, combined with the right action, will get your productivity to a level that few attain. If you don't do the important tasks that consistently need to be done, it becomes extremely difficult to build a highly profitable and successful business.

THE IMPORTANCE OF "RESULT RITUALS"

A ritual is something you do consistently with a proven track record of getting results. Some call them routines, others call them systems, but they mean the same thing. Once they're in place, they require little or no attention from you. "Result rituals" deliver predictable and consistent results.

> **The amount of stress you have in your life is in direct correlation to the lack of rituals and systems you have in place.**

Inside your business, there are specific activities that result in getting more customers, create more value for those customers, and sell more products and services to them.

I call these "profit maximizers" or "result rituals," which are the actions proven to produce profit for you in your business. If you do these key activities consistently over time, they result in more new customers that buy from your business, paying you more money. This results in a growing business, growing profit, and growing income. Some of these key activities include perfecting your product or service, testing and refining your marketing offers, and giving customers emotionally-impactful experiences, causing them to come back and buy more, and telling their friends to come and buy from you, too.

If you don't find ways to consistently execute on these actions every day, every week, and every month, you rob yourself of most of your growth and income over the long-term because you don't benefit from the compound interest these activities produce when done together over time. These activities create the most market value and result in the most profit and income for you. Almost every activity people do in their businesses are NOT profit-producing ones. This is a main reason why most businesses don't achieve financial success and why they don't create wealth, freedom, and financial independence for their owners. So, how do we turn all of this into leverage for you and your business?

The 80/20 Rule: 20 percent of all your activities account for 80 percent of your income. Figuring out what these activities are is the first step toward business growth. Think about the top three actions or activities that create income for you. Constantly ask yourself if what you're doing is profitable, and focus on doing what you should versus doing what you feel. Don't forget that impact drives income, and you're always paid for the value you bring to the marketplace.

What are the top three profit-producing activities proven to create results for your life and business?

Examples:

- Making sales calls
- Talking to your salespeople
- Writing and creating content
- Reaching out to companies or developing partnerships
- Making appointments, or even going door-to-door when necessary
- Sending emails to your contact list
- Creating persuasive copy
- Working on your delivery to sell more from the stage

- Perfecting your marketing message
- Creating a referral system for your business

1. _____

2. _____

3. _____

How much time do you allocate for these activities every week?

_____

How much time SHOULD you allocate for these activities every week?

_____

Track your business for the last six months. What 20 percent of marketing efforts have yielded 80 percent of the results for your current business?

_____

_____

_____

What 20 percent of people and activities produce 80 percent of my positive emotions and fulfillment?

_____

_____

_____

What 20 percent of people and activities produce 80 percent of my negative emotions and frustrations?

_____

_____

_____

Productivity is about what you do, but it's also about how you think. When you conceptualize importance and place a higher value on your time, you unlock an exhilarating level of freedom. Time is the stuff of life—it's the great equalizer, and it's all we have. In many ways, your productivity can single-handedly determine whether or not your life is a World-Class life and your business a World-Class business. It can determine whether or not your life and business are simply mediocre. It all comes down to how you manage your time, but more importantly, how you manage yourself and your perspective. How you spend your twenty-four hours each day determines your productivity. Make the most of your twenty-four hours starting now.

EXECUTION PLAN

What's messed up your momentum in the past? Clarify what's gotten in your way in the past.

_____
_____
_____

What prevention plan can you put in place to make sure this doesn't continue getting in your way? (If you don't have a plan to interrupt your interruptions, your plans will always be interrupted).

_____
_____
_____

What are the rituals and routines you are committed to that aren't negotiable?

_____
_____
_____
_____
_____
_____

What are the weekly tasks you do just to maintain your business?

_____
_____
_____
_____
_____
_____

What are the weekly tasks you do that produce growth for your business?

_____

_____

_____

_____

_____

_____

What activities can you either delegate or stop doing right away?

_____

_____

_____

What would life be like in the next couple of years if you focused on maximizing your productivity?

_____

_____

_____

_____

_____

_____

RULE 7

WORLD-CLASS LEGACY—HOW TO REACH SUSTAINED GREATNESS YEAR AFTER YEAR

UNDERSTAND THE BIG PICTURE

Entrepreneurship is one of life's greatest tests. More importantly, entrepreneurship both writes your legacy and sets it in motion.

It astounds me the number of entrepreneurs who don't spend enough time thinking about their legacy and what they will leave behind for their organizations, the people they serve, and their families. Leaving a great legacy is arguably the most powerful thing you can do in your career and life because it enables you to have influence well into the future—even after you're out of the picture.

> **The world's most successful people make decisions based on their legacy, not their current circumstances or mood.**

You can't build a real legacy with hype, a quick trend, or just money. Legacy is not defined by age or time served. Legacy represents your body of work, the people you've impacted, and the difference you've made in the world around you. Every piece of content, every social media post, and every conversation you have is part of your legacy.

I talked to a family friend the other day, and he shared that he was in the process of creating a trust for each of his grandkids. Most people don't think about trusts, let alone think three generations forward. That's legacy.

Throughout the course of this book, we've covered a wide array of tactics, philosophies, and habits that will help you achieve a World-Class lifestyle and truly live a life on your terms. So, how do you go about solidifying these new habits to ensure the changes are sustainable? It starts with having a pinpoint focus on your vision, one that resonates so deeply that every individual you talk to knows what you stand for and what you aim to accomplish. Someone with no vision for their future will always return to their past, and if you're too focused on your past, you'll take the present for granted and kill your future. So, let me ask you these questions:

- Do you have a mantra for the next twelve months?
- What compelling vision will drive you?
- What's your "magnificent obsession" going into the next twelve months?

When you can turn motivation into purpose or something bigger than yourself, you will achieve true, sustainable success.

As a child, I always wondered how famous or successful individuals stayed consistent, motivated, and hungry even after they achieved their dreams. In my eyes, they had everything: money, fame, cars, and respect.

So why did they continue to show up?

What kept them going?

Now that I'm older and I've experienced some notoriety of my own, I realize the meaning of success is forever expanding for all of us. There is no "peak" or endgame. Rather, we achieve goals and then habitually create new ones that align with our path. This is one of the most common traits I see among the world's best, although there are some individuals who experience a more jagged or temporary bout of success. What makes all of these people different?

Why do some people fall off and never come back?
Why do some fall off but later make a comeback?
Why do some never fall off?

Part of the answer to these questions comes from a recent interview I did with Tim Storey, a man who's been labeled the "comeback coach" due to his impressive ability to restore the reputations of America's former stars. When asked if there was a common theme among those who stray from the course, he responded by saying:

> "Here's what it is: lack of consistency. People suck in the area of consistency. They're great starters and have huge energy, but they don't stick with it. You've got to be consistent in all areas of your craft. As you've heard me teach, you've got to plow the ground. Plant the seed, water the seed, get the harvest. Plow, plant, water. It's one thing to be a great child actor; it's another thing to stay with the craft for years to come. It's important to keep the right team around you and continue to invest in your craft. A lot of actors stop taking acting classes. A lot of entrepreneurs—they just get caught up in what they can have as far as the cars, the houses, whatever. And I'm not saying there's anything wrong with that, but they stop being consistent."

In addition to the lack of consistency, there's also the fear factor. For some of us, the idea of success can be intimidating, or it's so far out of our comfort zone that we can't even envision ourselves at a World-Class level. We subconsciously choose to stand still where we are because, well…it's comfortable. However, complacency is the enemy of growth and growth is what drives progress. Only when you decide to take action and step away from your comfort zone will you finally start to feel alive. It's easy to continue living our normal, day-to-day lives while overlooking the need for growth or challenge.

It's easy to exist and coast on the status quo, doing what we can to survive and get by.

But do you really want to live that life?

This isn't to say that life isn't challenging; we face challenges every day. However, those challenges are often a result of something external or unexpected—something we can't control. By taking on challenges intentionally rather than waiting for them to occur, we can enhance the way in which we respond to them, making the challenges of everyday life much easier to deal with.

The best way to move forward in life is to create challenges, step-by-step. They improve our ability to rise to the occasion, regardless of the situation. And the tougher the challenge, the greater the chance for growth and capacity expansion.

We all instinctively know that anyone can accomplish something if they really put their mind to it. Anybody can be successful for a weekend, a month, and even for a year. We know this. However, real greatness requires something different: it requires grit and an unrelenting determination. You can't just show up when you feel like it or until you've reached a place that feels comfortable. It's a full-time job that requires you to be on the clock for most waking hours.

We've spent a lot of time discussing what it means to live a World-Class life, but what does greatness mean to you? Everyone has a different concept in mind, and defining your unique meaning is crucial in the entrepreneurial journey. Otherwise, you might find yourself pursuing someone else's dream.

So, with that, let's find your definition of greatness.

What does greatness personally mean to you?

_____

_____

_____

_____

_____

_____

What does leaving a legacy look like for you? What do you want your legacy to be?

_____

_____

_____

_____

_____

_____

THE EIGHT ESSENTIAL KEYS TO
UNLOCKING YOUR GREATNESS

Throughout all the interviews I've conducted during my career, and through the relentless studying and countless conversations, I've identified eight consistent themes from those who have built a World-Class lifestyle and become the top 1 percent in their chosen field. Four of them are about mindset and four are tactical strategies. By instituting these eight concepts into your own life, you'll not only be able to reach a new level of greatness but also turn your growth into a systemized process.

I. LEARN TO LOVE AND LEVERAGE FAILURE

Those who have reached greatness invested in the long-term, focused on their strengths, and always leveraged their failures. Look at every opportunity, whether you succeed or fail, as a chance to improve. As long as you walk away from your great failures stronger, smarter, and with a fresh perspective, they were learning experiences that prepared you to overcome and never repeat those mistakes again. There are certain things you didn't want to happen, but they did. The purpose of challenge and change is to make you different and help sharpen your perspective.

The very process of greatness means failing more often than your competition. That's just a fact. However, something phenomenal happens when you stay with your craft despite being continuously knocked down: you develop a thick skin. In order for this to happen, you must refrain from listening to your critics and get rid of any expectations created by others. You must block out the noise and stay true to your vision, despite the external distractions. Remember, failing is part of the process of building a World-Class life. A pro athlete doesn't become great overnight; he fails again and again until he can't fail anymore. By putting yourself out there and taking a risk, you will fail more than the ordinary person. That's just part of the game. However, you must reach deep within and do whatever it takes to bounce back. That's where the challenge comes in.

Successful people don't just enjoy failure—they welcome challenges. My good friend Tim Grover, author of the book *Relentless,* says 80 percent of success is emotional and mental toughness, and 20 percent is physical. The only way to become mentally tough is to take on more, not less. Don't let disappointment lower your standards. Instead, become more disciplined. Once you turn your disappointment into drive, there is truly no limit to what you can achieve. Success is an investment of persistence, and the more you invest, the better you become.

Don't believe me? Check out these examples of famous individuals who willingly challenged themselves despite having already achieved massive success and superstardom:

- Ellen DeGeneres returned to stand up after a fifteen-year break, despite having a $490 million net worth. When asked why, her response was simply, "I needed another challenge. I felt myself getting comfortable."
- Denzel Washington currently has a net worth of $220 million, and when asked about his career, he said, "I'm not competing against others. I'm just trying to get better. I act on stage, I act in movies, I produce, and I direct because I like new challenges. Challenges keep me young and on my toes."
- Jamie Foxx has a net worth of $120 million, and when asked about failure, he replied that he liked failure because it kept him humble and wanting more. He said, "Some days you get better, some days you get worse, but you learn more every single day."

In another one of my recent interviews with Robert Kiyosaki, author of *Rich Dad Poor Dad*, he said something that really sent this topic home. (Check out the interview on YouTube; it's one of the most powerful and controversial interviews he's done https://www.youtube.com /watch?v=bm4a3mX1cg0&t=1s). He said:

"In school, we learn that mistakes are bad, and we are punished for making them. Yet, if you look at the way humans are designed to learn, we learn by making mistakes. We learn to walk by falling down. If we never fell down, we would never walk."

Part of failing forward is focusing on experiments over perfection. Perfectionism is the enemy of entrepreneurship. Real entrepreneurship means committing yourself before you have the guarantee of success. Entrepreneurs begin to die when they start thinking about having a courage-free future. Think about the most meaningful breakthroughs you've ever had in your life. It was because you committed to something before there was a guarantee of any success, and that required courage. The difference between courage and confidence is that confidence feels really good, and courage doesn't. It's important to test all your crazy ideas, no matter how crazy they sound. Try them out. Find out which ones work, then optimize their effectiveness. Test all variations of that idea. Find out which variations work best and continue to adapt and adjust. Perfectionism cost me a lot of money early on in my career. When I decided to give up the need to be perfect in order to be authentic, everything changed.

2. DON'T ASK FOR PERMISSION

Great people don't ask for permission. Instead, they do what they need to do and then ask for forgiveness. If you want something, go for it. It may sound simple, but how often do we refrain from pursuing a goal out of fear of what others might think? We tend to wait to receive permission or validation as if we need the approval of our peers to run our business, careers, lives, and even our minds. In reality, you should be the only one holding the permission slip. You must shut out all of the potential judgment and just go for it. In time you'll start to learn how to generate your own certainty. Sometimes it takes becoming disgusted with the "old you" for the "new you" to rise up. With due diligence, the right network, and strong enough reasons, it becomes easier to go all-in without anybody's approval.

3. START GENERATING SUCCESSFUL TRAITS

High performers are constantly generating successful traits, while unsuccessful individuals think they don't "have" or possess these traits. It's not about what you have—it's about what you can generate. High performance has nothing to do with genetics. It's developed through practice. There's not a single person in this world who was born a success. Goal achievement comes with time, diligence, and the ability to harness the traits of the elite, whether it's clarity, energy, courage, productivity, or influence. They must be *generated*. A common problem I see among many unsuccessful people is they assume these traits are genetic or God-given; therefore, they believe they don't stand a chance. However, that's not the case. Whatever hand you were dealt at birth doesn't have to be the hand you stick with for eternity. If you have bad habits holding you back, you're fully capable of breaking them, just as you are able to gain productive habits to propel you forward.

4. DON'T PUT ANYONE ON A PEDESTAL

This may be the most clearly defined difference between successful people and everyone else. Those who reach the top do so by being a player, not a spectator. You must force yourself out of the stands and get onto the field, regardless of how intimidating the field might be. So what if your colleague has put in more time than you? You still have every right to participate as long as you remain humble, self-aware, and put in the necessary time yourself. One of the greatest things about humans is that not a single one of us has an identical genetic makeup. We each have unique skills and talents we pursue on different timelines, meaning there's no logical basis for drawing comparisons between one other.

A perfect example of this comes from a recent thought I had while watching an interview with the famous illusionist, David Blaine. This is a man who has truly mastered his craft to an elite degree. He has completed stunts that most people, including myself, would never have the courage to try, whether it be swallowing gasoline, going forty-five days without food, or spending two full days in a solid block of ice. Yet when the interviewer asked him what his scariest experience has been in the past twenty years, he said it was the time he had to speak in front of

500 people. Hearing this completely blew my mind. How could a man who's executed some of the most terrifying stunts in human history be scared of doing something I do on a regular basis? The answer goes back to what I mentioned earlier: because what's easy or effortless for one person is completely different for the next. Comparison is the ultimate misery, and this is why it's important not to put others on pedestals. Sometimes it isn't that people let you down; you just had them held up too high.

You can accomplish anything you set your mind to, but you must be willing to go all-in, make the necessary sacrifices, and most importantly, figure out what you're willing to give up.

So, what are you willing to:

1. Sell yourself on?
2. Go all-in on?
3. Become a master at doing?

Another example of unique exceptionalism comes from a recent interview I conducted with the Vice President of the LA Clippers, Kevin Eastman. He shared a story with me about a time when he got to speak with Kobe Bryant, one of the greatest basketball players in American History, who was also known for his intense workout sessions. Though when Kevin asked him about his workout habits, Kobe's response was: "I don't work out. Everyone works out. I black out." While he didn't mean he literally blacked out, he was offering up a small glimpse into what made him so exceptional. When everyone else did a specific thing to improve, he did it too, and then he did some more.

Kobe also explained his focus-method to master a skill and said: "I don't care how young or old the player is—if I see someone doing something I don't know how to do yet, I'm going to think about it. I'm going to ask them about it, then I'm going to try it. It might be a footwork thing, it might be a different move, but I'll work on it the same day." Kevin then asked him how long he typically works at new skills, and his response was simply "until." Not "four hours" or "six months," just "until." Kevin then asked him one last time, "until when, Kobe?" He responded, "Until it's mastered." In other words, he worked at a new skill UNTIL he had completely mastered it, no matter how long it took.

The best are the best for a reason, but they all learned from someone.

5. PRACTICE CONSISTENTLY AND DELIBERATELY

Practice does NOT make perfect. Practice makes permanent. If your practice is average, then it's more likely you'll be average. There's a state of passively knowing something, and then there's a level of performance you attain when you consistently PRACTICE what you know. The more you PRACTICE what you know, the better you get. Professional basketball players know how to shoot a free throw, yet they still shoot them every day, over and over again. Why? Because they're committed to their craft and continuously strive to reach a higher level of performance. They understand that complacency is the enemy and just because they've mastered a skill doesn't mean someone else hasn't mastered it better. You must force yourself to engage in deep, deliberate practice every day, not only to remain productive but also to solidify your mastery and confidence. As we discussed earlier in this chapter, the worst thing you can do is stop challenging yourself. If you achieve what you set out to achieve, then find a way to make it even better. Push yourself past your limits in every way possible, and in doing so, your limits will expand beyond what wasn't possible previously.

6. MAKE IT AN OBSESSION

I can't fully express just how important it is to have true, genuine passion for your craft. It's the fuel that allows you to play at a World-Class level and keeps you going even when everything else in your life is telling you to stop. You may have to make some sacrifices or nix a few time-draining relationships as you naturally would with any obsession, but that's just part of the game. Anyone who's ever achieved greatness did so by putting their skill or craft at the top of their priority list, whether it be an athlete, a musician, or a business leader. Here are a few examples of sheer, raw passion for a craft from some of our country's greatest leaders:

- Warren Buffet said the single most important factor in earning his millions was unrelenting focus.
- Thomas Edison was asked about the key to his success and he said, "Most people do many things all day, don't they? I just focus on one thing."
- Kobe Bryant refused to leave practice until he took 300 shots.

When you see someone who's being publicly idolized for their success, they're essentially being rewarded for the unrelenting hours of private practice and dedication they've put into mastering their craft. When you love what you do, it's much easier to stay invested for the long haul.

This is why I talked so much about making sure that what you do will keep you fascinated and engaged for the next five to ten years. When you're engaged and have a passion for becoming the best at something, you're always thinking long-term.

Broke people live day by day.

Those who make less than six figures plan week by week.

Those who make six figures plan month by month.

Those who make seven figures plan year by year.

Those who reach greatness plan decade by decade.

Those who have reached greatness think in terms of decades and have a lifelong obsession. They dedicate everything to one big mission.

Be Ultra Consistent

If we want to direct our lives, we must take control and be consistent in our actions. It's not what we do every once in a while that shapes our lives, but what we do consistently. Consistency is the DNA of mastery and a requirement for achieving greatness. This doesn't mean consistently focusing on your craft once a month, or even once a week—I'm talking about focusing on it every single day. Without consistency, the process of growth becomes staggered, which makes it nearly impossible to sustain. A few others benefits of consistency include:

- Building momentum and creating a barrier against bad habits
- Making your tasks measurable—you'll never know how successful you are with something until you've done it consistently for an extended period of time
- Creating accountability by setting a repetitive expectation, whether for yourself or your team

7. BECOME A PEOPLE DEVELOPER

A real leader is not someone who can develop the most followers; it's someone who can develop the most leaders. Do you know how to attract the right people? I don't mean peers—I mean individuals who can help you achieve greatness. As I stated previously, my rule of delegation is that if someone can do a task at least 80 percent as well as I can, then I delegate it to them. However, delegation is just a small fraction of building a successful team. You must also know how to lead, inspire, and create a culture of excellence. When others follow you because of who you are or what you've done for them personally, such as teaching them how to be leaders themselves, that's the essence of becoming a people developer. Being in a leadership role isn't about power; it's about serving your team and doing everything you can to add value. And believe you me, the individuals you help to overcome their limitations and shift their perspective will remember you for the rest of their lives. Companies don't succeed; people do. And once you know how to develop them, your business will grow to new heights.

So how do you become a great leader?

It's about mastering the "What" and "Why" and finding the best "How."

What do I mean by that?

Great leaders master:

- What they are doing
- What the movement is
- What the business represents
- What the culture looks like

They know:

- Why they do what they do
- Why the movement is important
- Why the vision is so important

And they know **how** to get things done by hiring the best. They find people who can supplement their weak spots by putting out great goals, compelling visions, and creating movements that people want to be a part of.

8. SYSTEMIZE YOUR GROWTH

> **The world's highest achievers don't leave their growth and success up to chance, hope, moods, or feelings.**

They build systems to ensure that each week, month, and year is better than the one before. If you want to do anything in your life consistently, you can't leave it to chance. You must create streamlined, achievable systems that fit within your life. We constantly see examples of this among the elite: they develop priorities and then treat them with the same importance as they would an essential need, whether it's working out every day, traveling every month, or spending time with their families.

Here are the simplest ways to make this happen in terms of pure growth.

Daily: The 5 x 5 Daily Ritual
Weekly: The Weekly Masterplan
Monthly: The Monthly Pause and Reflect Review
Sixty Days: The 60-Day Reality Check
Quarterly: The Quarterly Review

The 5 x 5 Daily Ritual

For 5 minutes in the morning, think through your day and visualize your perfect day. Think about your most important tasks and how you want to feel when you hit the bed that night.

For 5 minutes at night, go through how your day was and think about how you want tomorrow to be. Did you do what you said you were going to do? Did you stay focused on your most important tasks? What can you do better tomorrow? What went well today?

Doing this reflection for a total of ten minutes a day can make a big difference in your daily, weekly, and monthly progress.

The Weekly Masterplan

My weekly planning consists of walking through my priorities for the week for an hour every Sunday. Your schedule is a reflection of your integrity, and behind every millionaire, you'll find a very strategic and intentional plan. It's crucial to invest your past mistakes, errors in judgment, and experiences into your future success.

> **The more you sweat in peace, the less you bleed in war.**

This means those who prepare when nobody is watching are those who thrive in the spotlight.

The "trick" to productivity is deciding what you're going to work on other than in the moment and then practicing that high-value work over and over until it's natural, habitual, and automatic.

Some important questions I ask myself are:

Q1. What did I COMPLETE last week?
Q2. What went well, and what didn't?
Q3. Where did I waste time?
Q4. When was I at my best?
Q5. What am I grateful for?

BONUS QUESTIONS:
Did I do what I said I was going to do?
Did I add enough value to the marketplace?
What did I create that is contributing to my legacy?
Did I focus on the 20 percent of actions that create 80 percent of my results?

Did I think through my decisions thoroughly?

Did I follow up with everyone I was supposed to?

What was my favorite part of the week?

Did I eat healthy and feel energized throughout the week?

How often was I "in the zone?"

WEEKLY COMMITMENTS:

What must I get done no matter what to solidify a successful week?

Make sure your commitments are intentional and strategic. Tie them to monthly outcomes and ninety-day goals. Stop doing things you aren't completely sold on and don't take on anything new if you aren't 100 percent sold on it.

PROFIT-PRODUCING ACTIVITIES:

Twenty percent of all the activities you do account for 80 percent of your income. Figure out what those are before you start your weekly planning session. Think about the top three actions or activities that create income for you. Constantly ask yourself if what you're doing is profitable, and focus on doing what you should versus doing what you feel. Impact often drives income, and you're always paid for the value you bring to the marketplace.

NONNEGOTIABLES:

Your habits define you, and what you do on a daily basis determines your success or failure.

What are the rituals and routines you are committed to that aren't negotiable?

What MUST HAPPEN for you to continue creating results in your life and business, regardless if you're there or not?

Elevating Your Circle of Influence:

Who do you need to reach out to this week to elevate your thinking?

Who can help you reach your goals at a faster rate?

Are you associating with those who hold you accountable or those who let you off the hook?

The Monthly Pause and Reflect Review

The easiest way to create the perfect strategy is to review your previous thirty days. I have done this religiously for years, and it's one of the best-kept secrets to my success and that of countless others. Analyze your big breakthroughs and perspective shifters by focusing on these tough questions designed to extract the most important information from your previous thirty days.

> What were your top five wins from the previous month?
> What did you absolutely crush last month?
> What were your biggest frustrations and disappointments?
> What were the most effective ways you added value to the marketplace?
> What was your gross and net income? Did you surpass or fall short of your goal?
> What key relationships did you build or nurture?
> What did you do to stay adventurous and fully alive?
> Was there anything that messed up your momentum in the past?
> Is there anything you spent too much time on that didn't yield results?
> What obstacles will get in the way of your goals next week?
> Did you hit income goals and other analytical and measurable goals for last month?
> What were your top three income-producing activities from the last month? Can you double down on these activities or focus more energy and resources on these activities?
> What activities did you waste time on or did not produce the results as needed to justify the time commitment?
> Have a full team review for the past month focused on engagement, speed, results, communication, skill development, and so forth. What do they need? How can you help them?

The 60-Day Reality Check

Every sixty days, I eliminate "stuff" and increase energy. I recommend sixty minutes to go through each of these.

Eliminate every task that others can do better than you.

Eliminate everything that drains your energy.

Eliminate relationships that go nowhere.

Increase everything you permanently love.

Increase everything that produces growth and progress.

Increase everything that grows confidence and certainty.

If you do this for twelve months, you will get rid of eighteen things that have decreased your energy and increase eighteen things that produce growth, progress, and income.

The Quarterly Review

Most of us start each year with lofty goals and a lot of fresh energy. Too often, that energy begins to diminish after a couple of months or after some unexpected turbulence. Before we can move on to all the new and exciting things the next quarter promises, we need to take stock of where we've been, what we've accomplished, and what we may have missed. This important pause allows us to accurately realign our next quarter plans with our long-term goals. This is the importance of quarterly planning.

Keep in mind that as we grow and change, the best path toward our goals can shift (and if we're planning effectively, we'll always be changing our plans). Sometimes, even the goals themselves can shift. This is where quarterly reviews come in to help you stay on track. It's important to note where you started the year and where you started the quarter. This allows you to calibrate your measuring stick and ensure your evaluations will be accurate. This also helps you analyze your growth more efficiently. The first step in staying the course and/or adjusting with confidence is to make sure you deal in reality and look at your bottom-line results.

What were your major wins?

What were your major setbacks and challenges?

What would you do differently if you could start again on a clean slate?

The questions I asked in Chapter 7 (about finding the right vehicle) are questions I also ask during my quarterly review.

As we've previously discussed, the first step in transforming your life is getting clear about exactly what it is that you want. I had the honor of interviewing the great Brian Tracy, who is a famous motivational public speaker and self-development author. He talked about something called Zero-Based Thinking, which is a great decision-making technique he developed. He says, "When you begin to plan your long-term future, one of the most valuable exercises you can engage in is zero-based thinking. In zero-based thinking, you ask this question: 'Knowing what I now know, is there anything I'm doing today that I wouldn't start again if I had to do it over?'" No matter who you are or what you're doing, there are activities and relationships in your life that, knowing what you now know, you wouldn't get involved in again.

Zero-based thinking gives us the rare opportunity to ask ourselves if there is anything in our lives that we should do more of, less of, start, or stop. Tracy also says, "Top people are always open to the possibility and need for doing something completely different. They are willing to stop doing anything that no longer works or serves them. They don't get stuck in a 'comfort zone' and stay there just because it feels good. They are willing to take on the risks and the potential failure that goes with embarking on any new course of action." Use these growth hacks to systemize your growth so you don't leave your results and success up to moods or feelings.

I challenge you to avoid the common mistake of reaching a certain level and then getting complacent. Don't decide that you've reached enough success and then stop studying, learning, and growing. When we stop moving forward, we don't stay at that level of success; we start to slide back down the hill. If we aren't growing, we're dying.

Legacy building is part of the "big picture." It keeps us focused on the long-term and gives us values to judge our actions. Leaving a legacy for others is part of what drives me. I followed others who went before me because they left a legacy for me. All good men and women must take responsibility to create legacies that will take the next generation to a level we can only imagine. Ultimately, your legacy is all you've got. Think about how you want to be remembered by other people and act on those thoughts.

CHAPTER 13

THE WORLD-CLASS PRODUCTIVITY PLAN

TO GET YOU STARTED, I'M PROVIDING THE WORLD-CLASS PRODUC-
tivity Plan offered through our Game Changers Academy. Don't think of
it as another task in this book, but as the first course of action towards
achieving a World-Class life. This will help you simplify everything in
your head and create a straightforward plan. I believe in you. Now it's
time for you not to just believe in yourself, but to bet on yourself with
all you've got. It's time to get rid of all the noise in your head and focus
on what really matters.

If you want a copy of this plan in PDF format as well as a deep dive
video training of me explaining how I personally create my productivity
plan, you can download it at GameChangersMovement.com/Blueprint.

For this productivity plan, we use a six-month timeframe as a basis
for achieving your goals. Many books like to talk about ten-year, twenty-
year, and lifetime plans, which is great and all, but there are too many
variables. You change, plans change, customers change, markets change,
goals change, making it hard to stay the course all the way to the end
result.

It's important to have an overall vision for your life and business
for the next five to ten years, but it doesn't need to be exact. It should
include how you want to live and the ideal type of lifestyle you want.
Things should then be broken down into your ideal six-month vision

and articulated. In order to obtain your life-changing vision, you must focus on where you want to be in the next five years, articulate your ideal next six months, and plan what you must do in the next ninety days to accomplish that vision.

Start by considering the following question:

What is your ideal six-month outcome? If everything were to go right during the next six months, what would that look like?

Often when I ask this question to entrepreneurs, I get extremely vague answers like, "I want to make more money," or "I want to feel better," or "I want to be more successful," which isn't what we're looking for here. The goal is to be as precise and detailed as possible. You'll never hit a target you can't see, and if you don't know exactly where you're going, you'll most likely end up in a place where you don't want to be.

To really get your juices flowing, let's expand on the question a bit more:

Six months from now, if everything works out perfectly, what would your company and/or brand look like? Or if you don't have a brand or company, what would your ideal life look like? The key here is to base the answer on *your potential and what's possible*, NOT on your past or previous experiences. Don't let past failures or insecurities get in the way of what's possible.

> **The only way to live a World-Class life is to let your self-image precede your current reality.**

Start by listing what you want, what's ideal, and what's possible.

_____

_____

_____

_____

_____

_____

_____

_____

_____

_____

Once you create your World-Class vision, don't change it every couple of weeks. Most entrepreneurs are constantly scrapping their vision and rewriting it to try and obtain overnight success when there is no such thing. Create your perfect vision and stick to it. Keep grinding, and the results will follow. The goal is to let your vision guide you, not your current circumstances.

Now, what are your top five core values? What's important to you?

_____

_____

_____

_____

_____

Having a solid understanding of your values is important as these will provide you with motivation and determination during the most challenging times of your journey. The priority of your values may change depending on what stage you're at in your journey, but decisions become a lot easier when you've determined your values.

Some examples might include:

- Autonomy/Freedom/Flexibility
- Financial Freedom
- Adventure/Travel
- Legacy
- Health
- Contribution/Giving Back
- Family
- Impact
- Peace of Mind

List your top five values in descending order of importance:
What are YOUR "Big Five" for the next six months?

1. _____

2. _____

3._____

4._____

5._____

If we were sitting down six months from now, what are the five main things that would've happened for you to be completely satisfied and excited about your results?

1._____

2._____

3._____

4._____

5._____

Now we need to uncover the WHY behind your goals. When I think back to all of the goals I've set for myself, my team, my clients, and those I've helped, there's been a common thread among the ones that were achieved: the person striving for their goal had strong enough reasons to pull them through any challenge and keep them focused on their end result, regardless of the circumstances.

Reasons always come first; results come second.

Are you 100 percent clear on **why** you're doing what you're doing? If not, what can you do today to gain more clarity? This is your fuel and what will keep you going when things get tough. You'll need internal and external reasons.

What are the top twenty most compelling reasons for your pursuit?

1._____

2._____

3._____

4._____

5._____

6._____

7._____

8._____

9._____

10. _____

11. _____

12. _____

13. _____

14. _____

15. _____

16. _____

17. _____

18. _____

19. _____

20. _____

This might seem harsh, but those reasons listed above probably aren't compelling enough. You need something that wakes you up in the morning, a powerful reason that transcends any emotional desire to quit. You need a vision of something you're super excited about and allows you to serve more than just yourself. Which ones are the most emotionally compelling? Are there any that give you chills when you dive deep into the why? Jot them down below.

What are your *TOP five* most compelling reasons to hit YOUR "Big Five"?

1. _____

2. _____

3. _____

4. _____

5. _____

Now let's move onto the hard part: acquiring the skills to reach your ideal outcome. Being highly skilled in a specific area is a surefire way to achieve success in most industries. In fact, the skills you have are essentially your weapons, and as with any weapons, you must learn how to use them efficiently.

As we discussed in the previous chapters, the primary threat you'll face when it comes to mastering a skill is information overload, consuming too much, and getting trapped in the noise. There's also the battle of settling with "good enough," or learning just enough to get by and not pushing forward. While this might be a nice, comfortable place to sit, there's no opportunity for success in the space of mediocrity. Apple said it bluntly: "We shouldn't be criticized for using Chinese workers; the US has stopped producing people with the skills we need." Ouch!

That being said, answer the following:

What are the top three key behaviors or skills you must develop to achieve your Big Five?

1. _____
2. _____
3. _____

These should be skills that compliment your strengths and skills that are:

1. Proven and relevant skills that get results
2. Skills you are excited about learning and enhancing

Now you need to narrow these down from three skills to one. What's the number one skill you need to master to have the biggest impact on your ultimate goal? This depends on the stage you're in with your business and will change as your journey progresses. For me, one of the first skills I needed to master was networking. Then, it was sales, team-building, marketing, and eventually positioning. What's yours?

_____

From here on out, only study and consume information that is relevant to the above goals. All of the podcasts, events, masterminds, courses, and content you consume should be focused on that skill. No more random action, no more random personal growth. If you are serious about building a World-Class life, you need to move with more intention and purpose than ever before.

BREAKING DOWN YOUR GOALS

We've discussed your big goals, the reasons behind them, and the skills needed to achieve them, but how do we actually start to make progress? It's simple. Break your five main goals down into smaller, more achievable goals.

Some examples of this might include:

- Becoming the top salesman in your office for the week
- Saving your first $5,000
- Doubling your sales calls
- Speaking at an event or getting paid to speak
- Adding ten clients to your business
- Writing the first three chapters of a book
- Attracting your first affiliate or partnership
- Building your subscriber base to 1,000

Now it's your turn.

What are your top three goals for the next three months? These must be congruent with your Big Five for the next six months.

1. _____
2. _____
3. _____

Let's take it one step further and break them down even more:

What are your top three small goals for month one?

1. _____
2. _____
3. _____

What are your top three small goals for month two?

1. _____
2. _____
3. _____

What are your top three small goals for month three?

1. _____

2. _____

3. _____

Now, reverse-engineer from those goals and move backward. Set monthly milestones, and then set weekly action steps. Here's where mastery versus overload really comes into play. Before you consume any content, you must measure it against your Big Five above and ask the following:

Is this information relevant and congruent to my ideal vision?

Is this information focused on the number one skill I need to master?

Every podcast, book, audible, academy, and seminar you consume needs to be focused on that skill and those goals. When you get addicted to outcomes and results, you'll start to produce results like the top 1 percent. Amateurs are addicted to information and knowledge, but professionals are addicted to results and outcomes.

CHAPTER 14

THE BULLETPROOF IMPLEMENTATION PLAN + THIRTY-DAY CHALLENGE

> **If you try to change your business model, your fitness, your relationships, your network, and every aspect of your business all at once, you're setting yourself up for failure. You'll become mediocre in each at best. When you try and catch two rabbits, you'll catch none.**

FOCUS ON MASTERING ONE AREA OF YOUR LIFE AT A TIME, THEN move on to the next one. Improve your health, then improve your family, then improve your business, and repeat. If you go through cycles where you are continually improving different areas of your life, then the other two areas that are stable will provide the foundation you need. Complexity is the enemy of execution. True beauty is found in simplicity. Now that you have your productivity plan from the previous chapter, it's important you keep those goals at the forefront of your mind at all times.

As you move forward in building your plan, continue to assess yourself at the end of every week, month, and quarter. Twenty percent of your execution will lead to 80 percent of your results and outcomes. Each time you assess and move forward, invest more time in that 20 percent and less time in the last cycle's 80 percent. Develop an action plan that will take you from where you are to the life and greatness you know you deserve as a new Game Changer. Nothing works unless you do. Nothing that was previously discussed here will work until you put in the work.

Now, go through each chapter's action plan. If you haven't filled these out, please go back and do so. Don't be like most people who read books but never apply the knowledge and reap the rewards. Pick one action step from each chapter—one that's most relevant to the current stage of your life and business. Start with Chapter 2 and go through Chapter 12, but skip Chapter 7.

1. _____
2. _____
3. _____
4. _____
5. _____
6. _____
7. _____
8. _____
9. _____
10. _____

Now pick the two actions above that you feel would make the biggest difference in your life and business right now, based on your current stage. They need to be congruent to the Big Five you've chosen from your productivity plan. Remember, most things don't matter, and if you do something well that's unimportant, it doesn't make it more important.

1. _____

2. _____

Why would these two actions make the biggest difference?

_____

Now block off sixty minutes in your schedule within the next thirty days to review your progress. On that day, ask yourself these questions:

1. Did I execute the first two actions?
2. Have I seen measurable results?
3. What are the next two I'm going to take action on?

I challenge you to take these seriously and become more intentional in all you do. I can assure you that life is a lot more enjoyable with freedom, success, and wealth. Are you really living your potential, expressing your creative genius, and living an inspiring life? You're just as capable and deserving as everybody else, but understand it takes massive sacrifice along with the implementation of the *right actions*. This is the greatest time in human history for those who take 100 percent responsibility for their economic well-being. Commit to these tactics with the focus your life deserves, and continue to cement in your mind that you are always in control of your economy regardless of outside circumstances. Much respect to you and the progress you're making toward a World-Class life.

CHAPTER 15

BREAKING THE VICIOUS CYCLE

WHETHER YOU FINISHED THIS BOOK IN ONE SESSION OR COMPLETED it over time, I'd like to offer you my congratulations. You've now completed a very important step. You took action and invested the time and effort required to start building a life and business on your terms. For some, this may have been your first personal investment. For others, it may have just been another checkmark on your leisure list. Regardless of the category you fall under, you did something that many people fail to do: you started something and then finished it to completion, but more importantly, you invested time into bettering yourself. You made a commitment to yourself and actually followed through. This is the first piece of verifiable proof that you're completely capable of achieving World-Class status. Now, it's just a matter of keeping that momentum going.

I want you to leave this book feeling empowered and unstoppable. I want you to have the tools, motivation, techniques, and knowledge you need to achieve sustained success. I don't want this book to inspire you for just a day. I don't want you to get back online or grab another business book for another small bite of inspiration. I want this book to be an instruction manual that leads to consistent action. I want it to leave you going out into the world to implement the amazing things I know you're capable of.

For me, writing this book has been a long, enduring journey full of reflection, hard work, and most importantly, commitment. Significant life changes like becoming a new father forced me to reconsider my work habits and lifestyle. I no longer had the option to stay up and write late into the night, nor did I have nearly as much free time throughout the day. However, if there's anything I've learned throughout my career, it's that life doesn't always shape the way we expect it, but we do have a choice in how we handle the unexpected. We can let curveballs derail our dreams, or we can roll with the punches and adjust as needed. I'm happy to say I have and always will choose the latter, and I hope that for the sake of fulfillment and self-worth, you always choose the same.

I don't want to end this book on a negative note, but I do want to give you one last piece of insight to consider, which comes from a place of humble honesty: society in its current state is broken. This isn't to say it was ever in a completely "fixed" state to begin with, but we're now exposed to so much information at such a rapid rate—we now have many more distractions that can keep us from achieving our goals. We also have to deal with the constant exposure of seeing our peers' accomplishments, which inevitably makes us feel less-than. This is something that's been on my mind quite a bit lately due to watching my own son's development.

I distinctly remember looking at his ultrasound and feeling so in awe of how human beings are created. We all went through this extremely complex process, and here we are, all together, on this earth. Our parents get so excited about our arrival while family members eagerly share photos and milestones. There's so much wonder and expectation; they make so many promises about doing and providing the absolute best for us. We then spend our formative years exploring with eager curiosity and becoming fascinated with the smallest, most insignificant discoveries while our parents praise our every move. Then, somewhere along the line, those initial dreams and expectations are swapped with the fear of instability and a 9-to-5 lifestyle. Goals are diminished, and without realizing it, our parents fall into the vicious cycle of mediocrity and drag us into it as well.

How does this seem to happen the majority of the time? Better yet, what can we do to prevent this cycle from continuing to impact generations to come? Some of you might be thinking, "family becomes the priority, that's just what happens," or "life gets in the way," but why can't that be the motivation to live life to the fullest with your family? By succumbing to mediocrity and settling, all we do is set up our current or future family to fail. We're saying, "settle for comfort and then wait it out until the end," which is so far from the initial expectations originally set. That "bright future" we were promised quickly becomes an unreachable goal resulting in meaningless pursuits, continuous struggle, and a mediocre life that no one intended for us to have.

You now have the opportunity to break this cycle. I recognize that this may seem like a lot of pressure, but this is a potential turning point where the pressure may be necessary—even helpful. Pressure should be a privilege. You're the only one who has full control over your destiny, the only one who can set a goal, take the necessary course of action, and achieve what you set out to achieve. And like I said before, you've already proven you're capable of commitment, so what's stopping you?

Nothing.

When you think about and reflect on your life, it's important to realize that no amount of guilt can solve the past, and no amount of anxiety can change the future. All we have is now. When you put some real urgency into your life and realize you are closer to death now than you were when you started this book, you'll understand that NOW MATTERS more than ever before.

Most people spend the first half of their life saying they're too young and the second half saying they're too old.

There's nothing worse than living in regret and wishing things were different. Regret doesn't happen overnight, and it doesn't even happen in a week. It occurs after a series of bad decisions and a focus on instant pleasure, without any thought of the real consequences. No more postponing your life. It's now time to truly build a life and business on your terms. One that you're proud of and allows you massive freedom and success. Don't just do it for you, but for your family and for future generations. Don't do it for your first name; do it for your last. I promise it will be worth it in the end. You might need to remind yourself that what's too hard for most people is just right for you.

I want you to look in the mirror when you're eighty years old and know with certainty that you lived an amazing life, built a legacy you are proud of, and most importantly, did things on your terms. It's time.

ONE LAST THING

MAY I ASK YOU A FAVOR?

If this book shifted your thinking or inspired you at all, I'm hoping you'll do something for me.

Give a copy to somebody else.

Ask them to read it. Let them know what's possible for them if they start to value their dreams and goals over their excuses. We need them. We need you. Spread the word.

Thank you.

Peter J. Voogd

ACKNOWLEDGMENTS

I BELIEVE THE ONLY THINGS THAT CHANGE OUR LIVES ARE THE experiences we create and the people we meet along the way.

I've met some amazing people on my journey to creating a meaningful and impactful life. In the acknowledgments of my last book, I started with, "I don't know where to start, as I've been blessed with a long list of great people who have stood by my side." I still feel blessed with the people around me, but the list has been minimized. As my vision got bigger and my values got stronger, my circle got smaller. The older I got, the more I realized who really matters, who really doesn't, and who always will. Respect should be earned, not given, and I've been more selective than ever with who I've allowed in my inner circle.

I do want to thank my courageous and amazing wife, Kayla. It's hard for me to put into words how much I adore and respect you. It's very refreshing to know I have such a strong and compassionate woman by my side. Nobody has ever understood me as much as you do, and I couldn't do what I do without your love and support. Santana, my young king, you have blessed me in more ways than you can even imagine. The feeling of excitement and gratitude I get from being your dad every day is priceless. There is nothing I take more seriously than being your dad. To my unborn daughter, I can't wait to welcome you into this world and spoil you with love and attention.

To my mom and dad, you have played key roles in my success and have always let me be who I wanted to be. You gave me the ultimate gift: belief in myself. Words can't describe how much it means to have parents who have never tried to change me. Thanks, Mom and Dad. I love you.

To everyone leading authentically and with integrity, I respect and appreciate you more than you know.

BONUS MONEY MAKERS + USEFUL RESOURCES

AS A GENUINE THANK YOU FOR PURCHASING *7 RULES TO 7 FIGURES*, committing yourself to excellence, building a business that matters, and taking control of your future, I've assembled a series of valuable tools you can use to help maximize your entrepreneurial experience and your profits. Sure, I could have offered you some BS special report or free video seminar like most "online marketers," but I'd rather give you something practical to help you move your business forward and get you on the path to making immediate income. You can claim the $1,297 worth of free resources at PeterJVoogd.com/Bonus.

The Game Changers Academy: GameChangersMovement.com. The #1 Networking Community for Entrepreneurs, Sales Professionals, and Achievers. The all-in-one resource for those wanting to elevate their network, grow their business, and create more freedom and autonomy. Join thousands of other ENTREPRENEURS from all around the world. Your circle of influence will make or break you and is the most powerful force on the planet. As featured in *Forbes* magazine, Entrepreneur.com, *Huffington Post*, *Business Insider*, MSN, Yahoo, and many other international publications.

Our Lifestyle + Productivity Blueprint: GameChangersMovement .com/Blueprint. I mentioned this in the productivity chapter, but I wanted to make sure you took advantage. This is my way of giving back and helping my fellow entrepreneurs during these uncertain times. This Productivity + Lifestyle Playbook will teach you how to double your productivity without doubling your hours and gives you a clear system to become more focused and stop procrastinating.

OTHER BOOKS BY PETER VOOGD

6 Months to 6 Figures: This book has become a worldwide phenomenon, selling over 500,000 copies thus far. This book is "the fastest way to go from where you are to where you want to be, regardless of the economy." In this book, Peter walks you step-by-step through the fastest, most-proven, and effective ways to maximize your income and reach the six-figure mark as an entrepreneur. This book will help you create quantum change in the results you enjoy in your personal and professional life. For more information, visit 6FiguresBook.com.

The Entrepreneur's Blueprint to Massive Success: This book walks you through the thirty game-changing lessons you must learn to thrive as an entrepreneur and create an exceptional lifestyle. These are the lessons that have made the biggest impact on Peter's business success, lifestyle, and overall peace of mind. Available on Amazon and Audible.

The Achieving Autonomy Mastery Journal: The strategic 2-in-1 planner and journal that achievers use to maximize their days and create a life on their terms. We've developed a unique proven system that helps you organize, prioritize, and schedule what matters most to you. Available on Amazon.

ABOUT THE AUTHOR

Peter Voogd is labeled as the world's leading authority for millennials and entrepreneurs by Entrepreneur.com and numerous other international publications. He is the Founder of the prestigious Game Changer's Academy, which has become the premier networking community for entrepreneurs and leaders worldwide. He's a 3x international best-selling author, with his book *6 Months to 6 Figures* selling over 500,000 copies. He is the creator of "The Young Entrepreneur Lifestyle 2.0" (YEL) podcast, which is one of iTunes' most downloaded and listened to entrepreneur podcasts. Peter is a true innovator and trailblazer in the personal and business development arena and one of the most sought-after keynote speakers in this space. His *Ambition is Priceless* and *Know Yourself Motivational Album* series have revolutionized the way entrepreneurs consume content and stay motivated. Peter's strategies have been featured in *Forbes, Entrepreneur* magazine, *Huffington Post, Success* magazine, *Business Insider*, Time.com, Yahoo Small Business, Yahoo Finance, MSN, and many other international outlets and publications.

Starting his first business at the age of fifteen, Peter has an irrefutable sense of passion and determination. His experiences of success, failure, and undeniable achievement have delivered him from broke to multimillionaire before age twenty-seven. Peter prides himself on his greatest accomplishment of all: mentoring others and personally training nearly ten thousand entrepreneurs to succeed. Over 45,000 people have joined Peter's various personal development courses. Peter Voogd is revolutionizing the way entrepreneurs do business and helps millions of his followers to truly live life and business on their terms.

He loves connecting with like-minded people, and you can connect with him through the platforms below:

Instagram: PeterJVoogd
Facebook: PeterJVoogd
Twitter: PeterVoogd23

BOOK PETER TO SPEAK

Peter Voogd has been engaging and inspiring audiences with his visionary messages for over a dozen years. He's shared the stage with some of the biggest and best names in the business, such as Robert Herjavec, Gary Vaynerchuk, Keith Ferrazzi, Adam Braun, Lewis Howes, Eric Thomas, Les Brown, Mel Robbins, and many other legendary speakers. *Forbes* has lauded Peter's mission and expressed that "Peter's advice has helped thousands define their dreams and reach their business goals."

Having been a top 1 percent sales leader in multiple industries, Peter's been in the unique position of experiencing what it takes firsthand while also being fortunate to learn from the leading experts on human performance and achievement, such as top CEOs, revolutionary entrepreneurs, exceptional athletes, entertainers, and Olympic champions. This has allowed Peter to uncover and ultimately share the secrets behind these larger-than-life individuals' extraordinary success. Peter has organized what he's learned into frameworks and systems to create breakthroughs for others. Peter can relate to his audiences at a level most can't, which is why he is one of the most requested speakers in the industry.

Book Peter Voogd as your next keynote speaker and you're assured to maximize the results of your sales team and increase the growth of your company. To watch Peter's speaking reel or to book him visit: PeterJVoogd.com/Speaking.